CHINA:
A WORLD SO CHANGED

CHINA:

A WORLD SO CHANGED

C.P. Fitzgerald and Myra Roper

HEINEMANN

HEINEMANN EDUCATIONAL BOOKS LTD
48 Charles Street, London WIX 8AH

HONGKONG · SINGAPORE · KUALA LUMPUR
EDINBURGH · AUCKLAND · MELBOURNE · TORONTO
NAIROBI · IBADAN · JOHANNESBURG · NEW DELHI

ISBN 0 435 32992 8

© Thomas Nelson (Australia) Limited 1972

First published in this edition by
Heinemann Educational Books Ltd 1973

Designed by David Hornblow
Set in 10/11 pt Baskerville by
Dudley E. King
Printed in Hong Kong by
The Hong Kong Printing Press Limited

ACKNOWLEDGEMENTS

In preparing this book, generous help has been received from many
quarters. We would like to thank the many people who have given
valuable assistance, particularly the following: Mr Rewi Alley;
Mr Nigel Cameron; Miss Muriel Crabtree; Mr David Huish;
Mr Lee Tsung-ying; Miss June Mendoza, (who painted the
authors' portraits); and Mr Joseph Waters. For making available
pictorial and reference material and material which is copyright,
we are deeply indebted to the following: Art Gallery of Hong
Kong; Australian National Library; Australian National
University; *China Illustrated Review*; *China Pictorial*; *China Reconstructs*;
Eastern Horizon; *Eastern Sketch*; Embassy of the Republic of China
(Taiwan); *Evening Standard*; *Far Eastern Economic Review*; *France
Soir*; The *Herald*, Melbourne; Hsin-hua; *Illustrated London News*;
Le Monde; *Life*; *New York Daily Tribune*; *Peking Review*; *Punch*;
Spectator; *Sphere*, London; State Library of Victoria; *Ta Kung Pao*;
University of Hong Kong Library; *Washington Post*. In some cases
we were unable to trace the original copyright holder, and we
apologise for any infringement which may have occurred. Wade-
Giles romanisation has been used throughout, but we have, of
course, reproduced quoted material as it was originally published.

For Muriel, Sara and Sue

I have just drunk the waters of
    Changsha
And eaten the fish of Wuchang;
Now I am crossing the thousand-
    mile long river,
Looking afar to the open sky of
    Chu.
I care not that the wind blows
    and the waves beat;
It is better than idly strolling
    in a courtyard.
Today I am free!
It was on a river that the Master
    said:
'Thus is the Whole of Nature flowing!'
Masts move in the swell;
Tortoise and Snake are still.
Great plans are being made;
A bridge will fly to join the
    north and south,
A deep chasm become a thoroughfare;
Walls of stone will stand upstream
    to the west,
To hold back Wushan's clouds
    and rain,
And the narrow gorges will rise
    to a level lake.
The mountain goddess, if
    she still is there,
Will be startled to find her
    world so changed.

                    Mao Tse-tung

Contents

Time Line 1793-1972

1793 Lord Macartney's embassy visits the Ching Court in Peking.

1839 British sales of opium in China led to the First Opium War after Commissioner Lin destroyed over 20 000 chests of the drug.

1842 A defeated China signs Treaty of Nanking, ceding Hong Kong and allowing certain trading rights in ports.

1851–65 The Taiping Rebellion causes incalulable material and human losses. (When Manchu troops, helped by British and French forces, captured the Taiping capital, Nanking, in 1864, final defeat for Taipings was certain.)

1858 Treaties give West European powers and Russia rights of travel, trade, residence and missionary activities.
Treaty of Aigun gives Russia territory in Ussuri and Amur River area.

1860 Anglo-French forces occupy Peking. Russia acquires large tracts of Manchuria.

1871 Russian troops move into Ili region of Chinese Turkestan.

1894–5 Sino-Japanese war—China cedes Taiwan, Pescadores and Liaotung Peninsula.

1898 Russia obtains twenty-five year lease of Dairen and Port Arthur, and sundry mining and railway concessions.

1905 Sun Yat-sen founds Tung-meng Hui, Alliance Society, as an anti-Manchu revolutionary force.

1911 Chinese revolutionaries at Wuhan are successful. Manchu dynasty is ended and Republic of China is established. Soon after Sun resigns, for Yuan Shi-kai.

1915 During World War I Japan plans expansion into China and presents the Twenty-one Demands.

1916 War-lord period begins on death of Yuan Shi-kai and weakness of Sun.

1919 May Fourth Movement starts in Peking. First general strike in Shanghai. Karakhan Declaration by USSR offers restoration of Chinese territory and rights. Little comes of this.

1921 Chinese Communist Party (CCP) founded in Shanghai. Communist International representatives begin arriving in China. Kuomintang revives. Mao Tse-tung and Li Li-san working for the CCP in the countryside near Hankow.

1923 Soviet-Kuomintang (KMT) co-operation begins.

1924 Northern expedition to unify China and defeat war-lords begins.

1925 Sun dies; KMT Left and Right begin to split off; Chiang Kai-shek begins to rise to leadership.

1926 Peasant movements spreading, also Chiang's opposition to the KMT Left Wing and his CCP supporters. CCP divided on attitude to Chiang and KMT. Stalin expresses need to check peasant rebellion.

1927 Chiang still professes friendship for USSR and retains Stalin's support but in April he launches White Terror by massacring Communist workers in Shanghai. Similar massacre in Canton in July.
Autumn Harvest Uprising; capture and loss of Nanchang by Red peasant troops. Chingkang Mountains becomes Red base. Red Army founded.

1929 Red base established near Juichin, Kiangsi Province; some land-reform carried out.

1930 Changsha seized by Reds; held for two days only (the Li Li-san line). Chiang's encirclement campaigns begin. Chinese Soviet Republic is born.

The Mukden (or September 18) incident serves as excuse for Japanese aggression.

Communists declare war on Japan; KMT concludes armistice with Japan.

Chiang's last encirclement campaign drives Reds from Kiangsi. In October, Long March begins.

At Tsunyi Mao elected leader of CCP. Communists proclaim an anti-Japanese Front and urge all classes to unite against the enemy. Base established in Yenan.

Sian Incident; Chiang, captured by own generals, agrees to co-operate with Reds.

Marco Polo Bridge Incident enables Japanese to march south and enter Peking. Nationalist Government recognises the Red Border Region (Liberated Areas).

Wang Ching-wei sets up puppet government in Japanese-occupied Nanking.

Pearl Harbour brings US into Anti-Japanese War.

CCP carry out the rectification movement, Land Reform extended.

Cairo Declaration—Churchill, Roosevelt and Chiang Kai-shek ensure restoration of Taiwan to China.

USSR enters war; Japan surrenders; treaty of alliance between USSR and Nationalist Government. Marshall mission goes to China.

KMT–CCP war breakout; Reds seize Changchun, Manchuria; US airlift helps Nationalists take some major cities. Red Armies enter Manchuria. Land Reform starts again on wide-scale.

KMT victories; occupation of Yenan. KMT forces over-extended; garrisons cut off. General Wedemeyer arrives to report for US government. Uprising in Taiwan against the armies of occupation sent by Chiang.

Red Armies move to offensive; wide-spread defection and desertions by Nationalist forces.

January: Peking falls. April: Reds cross Yangtse. May: Shanghai falls. 1 October: Mao declares founding of the PRC. Chiang moves to Taiwan. Mao visits Moscow.

Wide-spread agrarian reform moves. Beginnings of reorganisation of commerce and industry.

Sino–Soviet Pact of Friendship and Alliance; Korean War breaks out; Chinese People's Volunteers enter Korea with US threat to cross Yalu River.

Thought Reform Movement and campaigns against corruption initiated. USSR returns Central Manchurian Railway.

First Five-Year Plan opens; agricultural co-operative adopted. China takes part in Geneva Conference on Indo-China. Mao and Kruschev confer on Sino-Soviet relations.

Bandung Conference and Five Principles of peaceful co-existence. Sino-Indian dispute looms.

Kruschev denounces Stalin at Twentieth Party Congress. 'Hundred Flowers' period begins. US rejects China's suggestions for cultural exchanges.

'Hundred Flowers' period ends. Mao in Moscow—'East Wind prevails over West Wind'.

Great Leap Forward begins. Tibetan armed revolt is put down. System of People's Communes approved by the Party. Sino-Soviet split increasingly evident.

1959	Sino-Indian border dispute worsens. USSR criticises Peking's position in this dispute. China bitterly attacks Camp David meeting between USA and USSR.
1960	Bitter attacks on CPSU by Mao and Chinese editorials—and on 'imperialism' in Asia, Africa and Latin America. USSR withdraws Soviet technicians. Period of economic difficulties begins, accentuated by 'natural disasters'.
1961	Chou and Kruschev clash in Moscow.
1962	Chinese troops prove superior in Indian border skirmishes then order 'cease-fire'. US assures Peking it does not support a Nationalist attack on mainland.
1963	Public exchange of hostile letters between China and USSR.
1964	France recognises Peking. Kruschev falls—Sino-Soviet dispute continues. China explodes first atom bomb.
1965	Lin Piao's article 'Long Live the Victory of the People's War' given world-wide publicity.
1966	China refuses to attend the Twenty-third Party Congress in Moscow. Many public attacks on 'anti-Party elements'. Great Proletarian Cultural Revolution erupts with 'big character posters' at Peking University and Mao's 'Bombard the Headquarters'. Red Guards begin mass-meetings and 'Little Long Marches'. Some senior Party members attacked. Chinese students expelled from Soviet Union.
1967–8	Cultural Revolution continues—Liu Shao-chi revealed as 'China's Kruschev—traitor and scab'. Lin Piao, 'Mao's closest comrade in arms' named as Mao's successor.
1968–9	Cultural Revolution fades out. Major reorganisation of educational system continues. Economic situation improves. USSR moves in Czechoslovakia condemned. Mr Sato declares Taiwan vital to Japan's security. Ussuri River–Chanpao Island clash with USSR border troops.
1970	Strong protests on growth of Japanese militarism. Canada recognises People's Republic of China.
1971	China admitted to UN.
1972	Vice-Chairman Lin Piao no longer seen in public. Okinawa reverts to Japan (which also claims oil-bearing Tiaoyo Islands). President Nixon flies to Peking. Joint Sino-US communiqué issued.

Preface

'The Past in the Present'

For decades we have been treated to a series of portentous quotations about China, from Napoleon's sleeping giant waking to shake the world and Kaiser Wilhelm's 'Yellow Peril' through Foster Dulles's duty to contribute to Red China's passing, Dean Rusk's slavic Manchukuo, and Mao Tse-tung's 'power growing out of the barrel of a gun'; though these have been somewhat muted since President Nixon's visit, the spectre of a red-yellow-tangerine peril is not wholly laid. It is, in fact, very much with us in a slightly different guise.

It is argued that since China has become an admitted world power and no longer fears Western attack, maybe she will begin to see herself, arrogantly, as the supreme balance-factor of world *realpolitik* playing off the USA and her allies against the USSR and both, in turn, against Japan, in cunning, self-interested shifts of emphasis. And what sort of influence, it is apprehensively asked, may China have on the third world of Latin America, Asia and Africa? Isn't the China model a very dangerous one for the rest of us?

Meanwhile, ignoring such power-politics speculations, Western businessmen are vying to share the expanding Chinese market both as buyers and sellers, for China's potential contribution to international commerce is inescapably clear.

Even the casual newspaper observer has become aware that the People's Republic is here to stay, and more perceptive readers suspect that she may be making major and seminal experiments in agriculture, education, industry—indeed, in social relations generally. But the average citizen, like the average politician, lacks firm outlines of the 'China model' let alone clear details of its working. Between China and the West has hung not so much Felix Greene's 'curtain of ignorance' as a curtain of misinformation, woven of anti-Communist fears, of time-honoured stereotypes of inscrutable Fu Manchus, and of sensational headlines about barracks in communes, Red Guards chopping off hair—if not heads —and the destruction of ancient art treasures.

America's twenty-two years of intransigent opposition to the seating of Mao Tse-tung's China in the United Nations not only prevented an invaluable exchange of views but ensured that the presence of Chiang Kai-shek's Taiwan continued to generate tensions and darken counsel.

The Chinese were, for many years, understandably reluctant to admit Western journalists after their offer for exchange visits by Chinese and US journalists was turned down firmly by Foster Dulles in 1952, and after the continuing escalation of the war on China's southern borders. For many years the limited number of diplomatic missions in Peking further militated against direct interchanges. The phrasing of Chinese official statements and of articles in her foreign language periodicals often seems fierce, almost comically exaggerated—'paper tigers', 'imperialist running dogs', 'ghosts and monsters'—while her political terminology often seems both obscure and repetitious, and her torrent of words on the rigours and excitements of the Great Proletarian Cultural Revolution did nothing to clarify international understanding.

Now, at the beginning of the 1970s, the position has changed greatly. The Cultural Revolution clearly did not rend the temple asunder but strengthened Mao's hand; China is in the UN and on its Security Council; there has been an almost unseemly scramble to clamber on the Chinese bandwagon as nation after nation, internal political colour regardless, has exchanged ambassadors with Peking.

Though governments and press attitudes slowly evolve and the world steadily becomes more and more the global village, China is still hard to understand, and the problems of intercommunication remain. But to an increasing number of people the attempt to grasp the magnitude of Chinese developments seems essential.

Many of these developments are, of course, in line with those of other Asian and third world countries, caught up in the ever-increasing momentum of late-twentieth century living and political change. But much of what is happening in China is different, not only in degree but in kind, from what is happening in, for example, neighbouring Indonesia, Thailand or Japan. The reasons for this are manifold and complex but two are outstanding. The first is the uniquely Chinese leadership of Mao Tse-tung, a major formative force of the twentieth century militarily, socially and philosophically. The very magnitude of the scale of Maoist experiments, the propagation of Mao Tsetung Thought, the stated object of changing men's hearts and minds, of establishing a new set of national values and priorities, of sharing an 'ongoing revolution'—all these are baffling to Westerners with their established political concepts and ingrained scepticism. The terminology of Mao Tsetung Thought compounds the bafflement. 'The boundless strength of the masses', 'democratic centralism', 'one divides into two': these, the everyday fare of China's domestic and foreign language press, confuse and alienate many foreign observers.

The second reason is the course of Chinese history in the last century and a half—years of agony and humiliation for the Middle Kingdom. Certain trends and characteristics of these years, culminating in the victory of the Red Army and the establishment of the People's Republic in 1949, continue to influence both the content and style of China's policies today. Philippe Devillers, French authority on South-east Asia, writes: 'What Mao has said, is saying today and will say tomorrow about the USA, the USSR, Vietnam, Socialism and culture, has neither meaning nor justification (and is therefore not comprehensible) except insofar as it relates to the experience of China and himself over the last sixty years. If he takes issue with the United States it is because the US helped Chiang Kai-shek. If he takes sides in Vietnam it is because he sees the US carrying out the same policy there as she did in China from 1945 to 1950. . . . If he takes issue with the USSR it is because it seemed to him that Kruschev had become the *de facto* ally of the US and Kruschevism seemed to be stifling the Soviet Union's revolutionary vocation.'

One can fairly add at least another six decades to Devillers' sixty years, for Mao's historical perspective is considerably longer than his own life-span. To understand these influences it is helpful—though an obvious oversimplification—to distinguish five main aspects of these hundred and fifty years of Chinese history: the impact of the West on China; China's relations with Russia; China's relations with Japan; the role of the peasant in Chinese revolutionary tradition; the role of the intellectual in that tradition; and the merging of these last two in the development of the Communist revolution under the leadership of Mao Tse-tung, himself both peasant and intellectual. The material in this book has been dealt with under these headings; and special attention has been given to the suffering of the Chinese people during the grim decades of war and foreign occupation up to 1949, and to their living conditions today, for it is, more than anything else, the contrast between 'past bitterness and present sweetness' that most illuminates the attitudes of the masses towards their present regime. For the first time within living memory the government has given China twenty-four years of peace and freedom from the foreigner.

This book will then, in a sense, present history in reverse. After a general conspectus of the theme, 1840–1972, each section will record the main events and attitudes of the modern scene, 1950–1972 and then show how far these are the logical—even inevitable—outcome of preceding decades, 1840–1950. But China today is so complex and fascinating that no all-embracing explanation or analysis is possible, and some differences of emphasis between the authors should add an extra dimension to the record.

This will be very much a picture book, for which both English and Chinese lore give authority. 'Every picture tells a story', we say; the Chinese—'One picture is worth a thousand words'.

The course of events will be traced largely by means of primary sources, contemporary accounts given by people who were involved in, or observers of, the events of their day. There will also be many quotations from Communist Party documents and from Mao Tse-tung's writings, since these have indelibly stamped this epoch of Chinese history. Illustrations—photographs, cartoons, paintings, documents—have been selected, wherever possible, from similar contemporary records.

This first-hand chronicling will make it possible to glimpse events as they struck a contemporary, and help to evaluate them with all the wisdom of hindsight.

Material has been drawn from Chinese—Imperial, republican and Communist—Japanese, American, European and Australian sources.

The Impact of the West

s to your entreaty to send one of your nationals to be
credited to my Celestial Court and to be in control of your
untry's trade with China, this request is contrary to all
age of my dynasty . . . Your merchants will assuredly never
permitted to land or reside here . . .' (The Chien Lung
mperor)

he ideological and social system of capitalism has also
come a museum piece in one part of the world [Soviet
nion], while in other countries it resembles a "dying person
o is sinking fast, like the sun setting beyond the Western
lls", and will soon be relegated to the museum.' (On New
emocracy, Mao Tse-tung)

1 The Impact of the West: Europe and the USA

If we take the early decades of the nineteenth century, during which an increasingly tense situation developed from the illegal import of opium, as the time when China was first seriously affected by Western pressures, the impact of the Western world on China is not yet one hundred and fifty years in duration. The issues which were important then have no significance today: the opium trade is non-existent, the system of rights and privileges imposed by the West on China was finally abolished during World War II and totally extinguished under the People's Republic of China, the Communist-controlled régime which is now in power. Yet this impact, in new and contemporary forms, remains a potent factor in the relationship between China and other nations. The Chinese attitude to the Western world is ambivalent, being composed of emulation and resentment. Modern science technology, media of communication and some aspects of government are admittedly of Western origin, but they are seen as part of contemporary world civilisation, not the prerogative of some few nations. To the modern Chinese these aspects of our society are no longer 'foreign', but accepted, adapted, and also re-interpreted to suit the ideology of the present régime.

On the other hand, the residual evidence of Western affectation of superiority, and above all of a political right to interfere in the ordering of affairs in Eastern Asia (not only in China), whether by military power or economic action, is strongly resented and rejected. Attitudes derived from a recent past, when these Western assumptions had to be respected, continue to inflame opinion and focus national opposition upon the policies of the Western world. It is not only that the pretensions of the 'capitalist imperialists' are denied—the nations which make these claims are no longer esteemed by the Chinese, who see the capitalist world as a doomed system, sliding down through decadence to revolution which alone could redeem it. While the scientific achievements of the West are appraised and adopted, the use to which these skills are put in capitalist countries is decried as immoral, outmoded and noxious. Science in the service of capitalist profit, of imperial ambition, military domination or racial segregation and oppression, is seen as a crime against humanity, and also as an attempt to perpetuate a political predominance which serves the interest of only a few and denies the rights of the mass of the people.

The modern Chinese also have to evaluate their own cultural heritage; how far it has been rendered obsolete by the development of modern civilisation, how far it was inimical to the aspirations and ideals of the present age, and how much should and could be preserved, revived, re-interpreted and rejuvenated to maintain a distinctive quality for the Chinese culture of the future. The recent Great Proletarian Cultural Revolution was essentially an attempt to come to grips with these problems and find a solution which would harmonise tradition and the ideology of the Thought of Mao Tsetung. Thus, there is ambivalence here also. The old culture was pervasive and universal within the Chinese world; some aspects were obviously confined to the literate class, who were also the feudal rulers of the land. Other aspects were more popular, or directly connected with the lives of the mass of the people; but some of these were also tainted by the corruptive influence of the scholar-gentry. Yet, in another sense, all was the product of the labour of past generations of the people of China, even if the fruits of their labour were appropriated by a small class of literate rulers. The people should now enjoy what their forefathers produced—the palaces, temples, works of art and literature, all derived from the economic power of the rulers which, in turn, was based on the exploitation of the masses. Some points of view which placed too much emphasis on the value of these fruits and too little on the labours of the masses have been rebuked and rejected by the Cultural Revolution. But the definitions are not yet clear, nor are the decisions final. Much of what was condemned may, in time, be permitted—when purified of its class content. Much was simply laid aside for a period during which the people would be educated to appreciate it for what it was really worth historically, rather than regarding it as a valid or viable model for modern manners and modes of thought. A realisation has always been evident that the old Chinese civilisation was a great culture, flawed by a bad social system, but nonetheless a proud heritage which could not be denied and should not be cast away.

If these are the present fruits of the impact of the West, the stages and phases of the Chinese reaction were many and very different from the final outcome. Until the second half of the nineteenth century the West—or the 'barbarians', as the Chinese saw us— meant in practice a few nations of Western Europe. It is important to realise that American influence in, or concern with, China, was not appreciable in the first half of the century. There was some trade and an increasing missionary presence, but policy and statecraft were little affected. It was only during this period that the USA expanded across the continent to the west coast of North America, and California. For the American people and their administrations, then located mainly on the eastern sea-board, the Pacific was still a remote ocean reached only after a difficult journey round the Horn. Britain, who had emerged from the Napoleonic Wars as mistress of the seas, had achieved complete naval dominance. Almost all trade with the Far East was in her hands. The earlier trading nations, Portugal and Holland, had fallen to third or fourth place and were more concerned with maintaining control of the colonial empires they had founded than with expansion. The French entered the scene, but Indo-China was their principal interest. Much later came nations from Northern Europe, but with the exception of Germany they sought no territorial establishments. Therefore, the West, in effect, meant Britain and France. This attitude long persisted in the minds of the Chinese people. As late as the 1930s Roman Catholic missionaries in the interior provinces were deemed to be French, irrespective of their nationality, and Protestant missionaries—even American citizens—were popularly classed as English.

The Chinese reacted to the aggressive actions of the British and French with surprise and consternation that barbarians should be able to defeat the armies of the emperor so easily. They had believed many absurd myths about the foreigner and his ability to wage war, but now found that there were harsh realities. The foreigner was not only a barbarian, ignorant of culture and indifferent to the ways of civilisation; he was also a dangerous barbarian The Unequal Treaty of Nanking in 1842 had to be accepted and some of the provisions which later generations of Chinese nationalists found very offensive, were not seen in this light by the contemporary rulers. Let foreign barbarians govern themselves with their own incomprehensible laws in areas—the concessions—set aside for them, which would keep them apart from the population; this seemed a useful and practical measure. Let the foreigners collect the Customs revenue; more was remitted to Peking than had been the case under its own management. Great resentment was felt at the proposal to establish foreign legations in Peking; this impugned the prestige of the Throne and was an innovation never before tolerated. It is perhaps the only provision of the unequal treaty which later generations found normal and acceptable. The ruling class learned little from the first encounter, and soon after 1842 were to be preoccupied for many years with the great Taiping Rebellion which shook the Throne and nearly overturned the dynasty. Before it ended, the Second Opium War (also called the Arrow War) led to even more formidable foreign incursions, including the capture of Peking itself in 1860. The new treaty was even more oppressive. Huge indemnities were demanded for modest loss and expenses. This did much to damage the weakening economy and saddled China with debt from which she was not to escape.

The Chinese now passed from feelings of contempt and fear to a new attitude. The great officials who had suppressed the Taiping Rebellion sought modern arms and started arsenals to make them; foreign weapons were recognised as superior and essential. The weapons of the foreigner were needed to repel the foreigner himself, but there was as yet no recognition that the military power of the barbarians came from more than this, no understanding of the background of science and technology which produced modern armaments. It was realised that it was no use merely buying foreign warships and guns; men must be trained to use these weapons, so selected young student officers were sent to serve with the British Navy and in European arsenals to learn their art. Some of these, the most famous being Yen Fu, soon understood that much more than expertise as a naval officer was needed if the 'secret of wealth and power' which the foreigner possessed was to be acquired by the Chinese. Virtually abandoning his naval career he devoted a long life to the translation into elegant literary Chinese of the works of the political philosophers of the West whom he considered best explained the real secret of the foreigners' power. Adam Smith, Montesquieu, John Stuart Mill and others, were introduced to the Chinese reader, and a growing impression was made by this first glimpse of the sources of Western civilisation. Yen Fu argued that only when China understood what these writers meant, and why they were important, would the secret of wealth and power be discovered. Wealth meant economic power on the national scale; power meant military strength, seen as the prime necessity to combat the incursions and pressures of the West. It can be said that through the changing phases and succeeding generations Yen Fu's message has become the guideline of all Chinese reform and revolution: wealth and power; by self strengthening, reform, constitutional change, anti-dynastic revolution, nationalism, and finally Marxism-Leninism, the search has gone on until at least power has been regained, and wealth, it is expected, will soon follow.

The governing class moved rather more slowly; they first saw the need for modern weapons, then they elaborated, in the second half of the century, the theory called *Ti Yung*, from the key words of the maxim 'Chinese Learning as the Base [*Ti*], Foreign Learning for Use [*Yung*]'. This theory meant that the fundamental teaching and education of Chinese should remain, as before, Confucian learning and traditional literature; Western technology and science, including mathematics (which had been neglected) should also be taught, for 'use'. This system was comparable to what European education would have become if all children and students studied the Greek and Roman Classics as their main discipline, but, even if they were to be engineers, physicists or doctors, only studied the sciences as additional, secondary subjects. It was an inadequate intellectual response to an increasingly critical situation, yet in certain ways it has remained, if no longer acclaimed under its old name, one of the preconceptions of the Chinese outlook. Chinese learning might change, Confucius might be dethroned; Sun Yat-sen, the apostle of Nationalism, might take his place, and be followed by the writings of Chiang Kai-shek, and then Mao Tsetung Thought; but all these developments are certainly Chinese learning. They may draw from foreign sources but they produce a Chines product, and they successively became the orthodoxies of the Chinese people—the Chinese learning which is the base. The foreign learning, science and technology to which later ages added political science, economics and language studies, are still primarily for 'use'—for transforming the old Chinese society and for building a new one, but always under the direction emanating from the 'base', which is the philosophic interpretation of society, its aims and its needs formulated by the Chinese reforming or revolutionary leader of the day.

A simple, if often ignored fact illuminates this continuing process of selection of what is for 'use'. Galleries containing important or significant collections of Western art do not exist in China today; neither did they exist in the past (that is, before the Communists came to power) and there were no Chinese counterparts to the wealthy Western private collector. A few Chinese who have lived long abroad have acquired a deep appreciation of the qualities of Western art, but the nation, as a whole, has been untouched. Here Chinese learning, or art, holds the field; there is no apparent 'use' in Western art. The same can be said, in varying degrees, of many other aspects of Western culture. The Chinese have not devoted their talents to research into Western or West Asian history; their own suffices, and a general knowledge of that of the rest of the world is all that is required. It is true that much the same can be said of the average educated Western man, but for a long time past we have had our specialists devoted to the study of Chinese history and culture in all its aspects. The current tendency in China for the works of Mao Tse-tung to take precedence, at least in study and practice, over those of Marx and Lenin, illustrates the same strong bent towards the national culture.

By the end of the nineteenth century the Chinese had fully recognised that Western learning, far beyond the narrow confines of military equipment or technology, was of 'use'—indeed of vital importance. Students went abroad to 'drink foreign ink' in ever-increasing numbers. They acquired not only technical skills but also new and revolutionary ideas. They returned dissatisfied with the weakening dynasty, the conservative scholars who supported it, and the whole apparatus of the old Confucian state. Reform graduated swiftly into revolution. By now there were other models than the old imperialist countries of Western Europe, although these still attracted many students.

In the second half of the nineteenth century the United States of America entered the Far East with increasing influence; the impact of America began. It was not entirely the same as that of the Western European countries. America was not a colonial, empire-building country—even if some scraps of empire came her way more or less fortuitously. America had no concessions in China: her citizens made good use of the ones established by the Western powers. They also shared in extraterratorial privileges, but on the whole the USA was seen more as a cultural force than as a military threat. America became the goal of the Chinese student who could afford to get there. Yet it is clear that the impact of America was not what many Americans hoped it would be, nor what they might expect. The people of America subscribed large sums to maintain Christian missions in China; but though these establishments set up many schools, some universities and also hospitals, they did not convert to Christianity any significant proportion of the Chinese people. The schools were well attended, and the universities also; the sick flocked to the hospitals; but the purpose was to learn English and modern disciplines, science, technology and medicine. American culture was for 'use'; it did not become a 'base'.

There were aspects of the American way of life which made no appeal in China, and in the end provoked resentment. American racial attitudes, not only to their own Negroes but to Asians and therefore to Chinese, were resented. The first boycott of foreign goods organised in China was directed against the Americans and caused by the passage of the exclusion laws limiting Chinese immigration into the USA. In American life law is an all-important activity; the Constitution is a legal document, the power of the Courts is great, if not paramount. In China, law in this sense is not part of the cultural heritage; law meant criminal law for punishment —often harsh—of crime. Civil law was the affair of arbitrators, guilds, family elders, clansmen and village leaders, merchant guilds and professional associations. The state took no part in it and exercised no jurisdiction in this field. Consequently the political institutions of the US were never much admired—or probably understood—by the majority of those who studied in the US and returned to China. Even Dr Sun Yat-sen, educated in his early youth in Hawaii, framed his constitution for the republic much more on French than on American lines. American federalism, a key concept in the US, was seen in China as a dangerous and devisive system which would destroy the unity of the state which, even under the republic in all its phases, was as devoted to the unity of the former empire as any dynasty had ever been.

America was seen as a good friend in the years following the fall of the Manchu dynasty—a country which was opposed to colonialism and imperialism, a safeguard against the unrepentant Europeans and the new menace of Japan. But it was not regarded as a model for the new China. Lip service may have been paid to American ideals of democracy and liberty, but practice did not conform, not only among the military rulers of the early republic but also under the one-party rule of the Nationalists from 1927 onwards. When America brought down the Japanese Empire and found herself, overnight, residuary legatee of that fallen power, and also heir to the waning imperialist power of the European nations in China, opinion moved very swiftly against the USA. The Nationalists were disillusioned, and although dependent on American support, did not receive enough to keep them in the field. The Communists regarded America as the arch-capitalist imperialist power, their sworn and unrelenting enemy. Consequently, the American values were now discredited. Capitalism, rather than democarcy, or liberty, was the hallmark of the 'neo-colonialist imperialists'. They opposed the Peoples' Republic and refused it recognition. They sustained the Nationalist rump in Taiwan; they opposed the reunion of Korea under the Communist North Korean régime, they defended the French colonial power in Vietnam, and then intervened themselves. Everywhere, America opposed China, denied her rights, as at the United Nations, and supported her enemies.

Thus, the impact of the West ran through several phases in these one hundred and fifty years, but in some respects it was a circular movement. The Western barbarian was at first scorned, then feared, next emulated, then criticised, and now is, in fact, once more discredited. The current conviction is that the 'imperialists are paper tigers', in Mao Tse-tung's famous phrase; fearful to look upon but harmless and even ridiculous in fact. They are riddled with contradictions; their society is rotten and degenerating, their people have turned away from their rulers, and there is no accepted ideology; it is a society in decay. Only revolution can restore it. Thus China once more stands forth, as the Manchu rulers formerly but vainly believed, as in truth the leader of the coming age, in which the Thought of Mao Tsetung will be the new orthodoxy, the guiding star for the dark world beyond the light of Chinese civilisation. That civilisation must itself be reshaped, casting away what is out of date and evil, keeping what springs from the People, the sole source of strength and cultural advance. The impact of the West has had the effect of a collision rather than a collaboration. In that collision both sides have suffered damage. China saw herself imposed upon, invaded and oppressed for more than a century, and the experience has left a trauma which will not swiftly pass away. The West has suffered, even if not so apparently or directly.

The beliefs of the nineteenth century are now as wholly discarded among the peoples of Western Europe as the outlook of Confucian mandarins in China. The loss of empire is not regretted by the young, and hardly mourned by the elderly. The confidence which inspired Christian missionaries with the belief that China—as elsewhere—could only be saved by conversion has wholly disintegrated; the once universal opinion that the institutions of the West were the only viable and proper forms of government is doubted even at home, and devalued abroad. How far these changes are in part a consequence of the turbulent relationship between the Western world and China can hardly be assessed; but it would seem probably that in the future the influence of the Chinese Revolution and of the leadership of Mao Tse-tung in its later phase will be seen to have been one of the great formative factors in shaping human society in the next century.

To China in the 1970s Europe no longer seems the enemy from the West, but for two decades after 1949 the relations between the new Chinese People's Republic and Western Europe, especially the United Kingdom and France, were tenuous, and exchanges were few. Britain 'recognised' the People's Republic of China in 1950 but full ambassadorial exchanges were precluded by the British government's ambivalent attitude on the status of Taiwan where it maintained a minor consulate, primarily for trade purposes. France, involved in a bloody war to retain her colonies in Indo-China, was, until the decisive defeat at Dien Bien Phu, an only too flagrant example of hated Western imperialism, lingering on after its time, and de Gaulle was vigorously 'anti-Red'. *China Pictorial* declared in 1968 that 'Europe and North America are the age old lairs of the imperialists; US-led imperialism has always regarded these [European] regions as its solid rear area where it exercises the strictest control. Armed with Mao Tsetung Thought the 700 million Chinese people stand firmly on the side of the revolutionary people of Europe'.

Both countries were despised as 'running dogs of American imperialism', rather than feared. The only echoes heard of past relations with Britain were when the British government and Chinese Communists clashed during the Cultural Revolution period in Hong Kong, the last outpost of British overlordship on Chinese soil. The clash had been precipitated by the jailing of several Hong Kong Communist journalists. In reprisal, Red Guards burned down part of the British Embassy in Peking and manhandled some of its diplomats.

From time to time the *People's Daily* comes out with a stern reminder to Westminster that Hong Kong was taken from China by yet another unequal treaty and the continued existence of the colony is, by implication, an act of grace and favour with no guarantee of continuity. Peking offers lusty verbal support for Britain's and France's 'revolting' students, and receives with considerable ceremony revolutionary delegations from Marxist-Leninist parties in both countries.

But in spite of such outbursts, China has moved slowly towards closer and happier relations with Western Europe. The Red Guards were reprimanded for their arson and the embassy building repaired at Chinese expense. The situation improved markedly when, in 1971, Britain unreservedly stood for China's admission to the United Nations, opposing American moves for delaying procedures and, soon after, issued a statement including an all-important paragraph on her recognition of Peking's sovereignty over Taiwan.

After Britain and China signed their agreement a joint statement was released confirming 'non-interference in each other's internal affairs' and the two governments 'decided to raise the level of their respective diplomatic representatives in each other's capital from chargé d'affaires to ambassadors as from 13 March 1972'.

'The Government of the United Kingdom recognises the Government of the People's Republic of China as the sole legal government of China.

'The Government of the People's Republic of China appreciates the above stand of the Government of the United Kingdom.'

Both the British Foreign Secretary, Sir Alec Douglas-Home, and the new ambassador commented further. Sir Alec Douglas-Home told the House of Commons that Britain acknowledged that Taiwan was a part of the People's Republic of China and held the view that Taiwan should be restored to China. 'We think the Taiwan question is China's internal affair to be settled by the Chinese people themselves,' he told questioners. After the signing ceremony Mr Addis (the ambassador) said: 'We have wanted this for a long time, really since 1950—our original recognition.'

France's unofficial links with the Chinese have been more sympathetic in many ways than those of Britain. Several of the Chinese Communist Party leaders were students in France; both Chen Yi and Chou En-lai learned their first Communist lessons there. Therefore, de Gaulle's decision to 'recognise' the People's Republic of China in 1964 was given a warm welcome, and since then Peking has been visited by some of France's most distinguished scholars and politicians, including ministers such as M. André Bettencourt and M. Couve de Murville. On his return from China, the latter said in *France Soir* on 20 November 1970: 'For the first time in more than a hundred years China again found its unity, the Chinese people were brought together again, a government established control of the whole country taking its destiny into their own hands; an event of cardinal importance in the history of the world, the consequences of which we can as yet only imagine. For forty years Mao Tse-tung has been the physical embodiment of the [Communist] doctrine. He received me for an hour and a half . . . a man of seventy-eight years who, after thirty years of revolutionary struggle, still remains uncomplicated, robust and alert.'

For the People's Republic of China the real enemy from the West was the USA which the Communists found as intransigently opposed to them after 1949 as before. For two decades China suffered from US isolation and containment policies. US bases are still to be seen wherever she looks across her coasts and her southern border. Spy-planes have been shot down deep in Chinese territory. For years she believed that the USA was grooming Japan to take over her role in the US drama where Asians were to fight Asians.

When the Korean War broke out in 1950 and the UN forces moved across the 42nd parallel into North Korea, China saw the UN troops as another 'puppet army'. Peking warned Washington and the United Nations against the threatened crossing of the Yalu River border and waited for several weeks before calling for volunteers to meet the threat of General Macarthur's armies. Finally, Chinese troops met the challenge with force, were successful, then returned home. China still bitterly resents the UN branding of her actions in Korea as aggressive and sees this action, also, as United States' malice and manipulation. For years she insisted that this decision should be rescinded before her own entry into the United Nations.

Even more bitterly has China resented the USA's continuing military, economic and moral support for the 'Chiang Kai-shek clique' on Taiwan. 'We must liberate Taiwan' has been a popular slogan, and Chiang's oft-repeated promise to the Nationalists that he would (with US help) retake the Mainland from the 'red bandits' seemed for some time more than an empty threat.

To Peking, America's role in the Vietnam tragedy is the most flagrant act of latter-day imperialism, but, she says, the USA will be devoured, like France, in the flames of the Vietnam people's war. 'Vietnam and China', said Chou, 'are as close as the lips and the teeth', and he offered warm support to Hanoi.

To China it was always clear who delayed her entry into the United Nations for twenty-two years and she sees American imperialism as a threat not only to her but to all 'newly emerging forces', the third world of Asia, Africa and Latin America. Certainly, innumerable pronouncements of the US State Department, members of Congress and virtually the entire US press, gave China firm foundations for her fears and her indignation right up to the Nixon visit of 1972, and indeed, thereafter. As late as 1966 Dean Rusk was taking almost the same hard line as John Foster Dulles before him. 'We must take care to do nothing which encourages Peking, or anyone else, to believe that it can reap gains from its aggressive actions and designs. It is just as essential to "contain" Communist aggression in Asia as it was and is to contain Communist aggression in Europe.' As late as September 1971 the United States seemed to make a last-ditch stand against China's admission to the UN.

China has seen Western 'economic imperialism' as no less vicious than its military variety and she uses all her very considerable propaganda machinery to lambast it. She believes that the capitalist system, developed by Western Europe and taken over by the United States, is collapsing, that Europeans and Americans alike will have to go home from foreign boardrooms and banking houses as well as battlefields and bases and the greatest capitalist of them all will have the hardest fall.

Foreign Minister Chen Yi commented bitterly from time to time on US economic and military activities limiting Chinese trade. US economist, Alexander Echstein, wrote in his book *Economic Growth and Foreign Trade*: 'Since 1950, US policy on trade with China has involved a virtually total embargo on all economic contacts between ourselves and the Mainland and the maintenance of as stringent controls as possible on trade between our allies and the Mainland . . . US policy toward China in effect is designed to isolate it and to contain it within its boundaries and trade controls are intended to support both these objectives.'

On China's domestic front, American China-watchers' voices consistently prophesied woe: 'The food intake of the Chinese peasantry has risen from the starvation level of 1 400 calories to the simple-misery level of 1 700 calories a day. But those who have experienced life in an internment camp—the nearest thing to life in present-day China—will know how much even such a trifling improvement can mean . . . a "no-exist" situation is the present situation of Communist China today.' Thus spoke Joseph Alsop from Hong Kong in the late 1960s. Peking echoed the message, prophesying disaster to the USA in turn. Hsin-hua commented in August 1971: 'The US government has tried in vain to regain prosperity for the ailing US monopoly, capitalist economy. . . . But the state of affairs in the first half year shows that [it] has failed to shake off the worsening financial and economic crisis and is sinking deeper into the quagmire of the crises.'

Mao pointed out that China had also suffered from a more subversive American activity—spiritual aggression carried out in secular as well as church institutions. 'For a very long period, US imperialism laid greater stress than other imperialist countries on activities in the sphere of spiritual aggression, extending from religious to "philanthropic" and cultural undertakings. . . . Many well-known educational institutions in China, such as Yenching University and Peking Union Medical College . . . were established by Americans.

The Chinese are determined that Western cultural influences shall be minimal: in China there is no rock an' roll, no 'in-gear', no Coca-Cola for the young, no foreign educational institutions and no foreign investment. Western science and technology, a world heritage, must be sinified where necessary. 'We must walk on two legs' but walk in the direction that the Chinese people themselves decide.

But with the United States, as with Europe, China has given proof of the flexibility of her policies. She claims to abate not one jot or tittle of her opposition to any form of imperialism yet Mao has been saying from the first that co-existence between states of different political beliefs is not only possible but essential, so leaders must negotiate, however warily, and people-to-people exchanges are always desirable. As early as 1949 Mao hopefully said that 'Some ties between the Chinese and American peoples still remain, and, through the efforts of both peoples, these ties in the future could develop to the point of "very close friendship", but because of the obstruction of reactionary elements in both China and America, these relationships, in the past and now, are being greatly hampered'.

And from the United States even Dean Rusk, in the 1960s, began to respond: 'We have gradually expanded the categories of American citizens who may travel to Communist China. American libraries may freely purchase Chinese Communist publications. American citizens may send and receive mail from the Mainland. We have in the past indicated that if the Chinese themselves were interested in purchasing grain we would consider such sales. We have indicated our willingness to allow Chinese Communist newspapermen to come to the United States.'

Then, in 1970, out of the blue, American and European ping-pong players were invited to vist China and journalists were welcomed; Dr Kissinger flew to Peking, and in February 1972, his President followed in an unequalled blaze of world-wide publicity.

In his toast at the welcoming banquet Chou En-lai said: 'The peoples of our two countries have always been friendly to each other. But owing to reasons known to all, contacts between the two peoples were suspended for over twenty years. Now, through the common efforts of China and the United States, the gate to a friendly contact has finally been opened. . . . We hope that, through a frank exchange of views between our two sides to gain a clearer notion of our differences and make efforts to find common ground, a new start can be made in the relations between our two countries.'

President Nixon responded in kind: 'We have at times in the past been enemies. We have great differences today. What brings us together is that we have common interests which transcend those differences. As we discuss our differences, neither of us will compromise our principles.'

The cautious, carefully-worded joint communiqué issued at the end of the visit marked not only a new era for Sino-US relations and end of the cold war, but a major shift in the world balance of power, greatly affecting the USSR and Japan as well as the two signatories. The references to Taiwan are of crucial importance.[1]

President Nixon referred to 'a week that changed history' but one should note that his visit did not inhibit the Chinese from their fiercest brand of criticism. 'The situation in the US today is one in which "the gale is raging and the storm is about to burst". The struggle of the world's people against the US imperialism is surging forward irresistibly. The further decline and decay of US imperialism are inevitable.'

Chou En-lai flew to Hanoi to assure the Vietnamese that Peking would support them as firmly as ever, condemn the US presence there and seek as energetically as before to oust them.

But Western technology and Western skills could not be dispensed with. Initially the sheer burden of establishing the simplest apparatus of living demanded that the government use any experts they could find; virtually all had been trained in Western-style institutions, so for a long time teaching and practice had to continue on Western lines. It is foreign 'scientific ink' that the Communists have most avidly drunk from their earliest days. However, as Mao's influence increased, they accepted his repeated warnings that they must not follow Western scientific theories and techniques slavishly but use them as a means of developing Chinese methods and institutions—'We must walk on two legs', that is, Eastern and Western, traditional and modern. From the best of each a new synthesis must emerge; Western science was to be sinified. Later, in some fields at least, they believe China will no longer follow and adapt, but lead and initiate. As Mao said: 'Dare to think and dare to do; break conventions; try to make use of the world's existing scientific and technical achievements. . . . We shall surpass world levels by a series of Five Year Plans . . . constructing our country as a Socialist power armed with first-rate science and technology.' The sophistication of China's atomic bombs was a spectacular example of China's firm grasp of Western science and technology. In the applied sciences she has been especially successful and the resulting achievements in industry, medicine, communication and transport are impressive.

One of the most dramatic and, to Westerners, the most esoteric example of Chinese science 'walking on two legs' has been the adaptation of acupuncture for anaesthesia. There has also been a great drive to encourage peasants and soldiers to study and collect the traditional herbs of the centuries-old pharmocopeia, which are now being investigated in medical research institutes. The Academia Sinica has invited increasing numbers of Western scientists to visit hospitals and their reports on the acupuncture and the experiments in modern uses of herbal medicines are arousing great interest and inquiry.

Anti-colonialist activities in Hong Kong: Red Guards dismantle a clock and watch shop sign which they feel is tinged with colonialism. (*China Pictorial*)

Tram workers and Hong Kong riot police. 'Under the guidance of Mao Tsetung's Thought, our patriotic compatriots in Hong Kong and Kowloon are . . . getting organised and are courageously and fiercely unfolding struggles against the vicious British imperialism. They are ready at any time to respond to the call of the great motherland to smash the reactionary rule of the British imperialism in Hong Kong.' (*China Pictorial*)

'Since last May the students and teachers of France have stirred up a widespread and vigorous student movement to oppose the existing decadent educational system and the reactionary policies in both domestic and foreign affairs enforced by the French ruling clique.' (*China Pictorial*)

M. André Bettencourt of France greeting Mao Tse-tung. 'The good relations between our two countries have been growing day by day . . . The people of both China and France have a revolutionary tradition. Though they have different social systems, our two countries cherish independence and oppose control and interference by super powers.' (Kuo Mo-jo, Vice-Chairman, National People's Congress, speaking on the same occasion)

Soldiers from the Chinese People's Liberation Army which fought the United States of America in North Korea.

Chou En-lai (centre) and other members of the Chinese delegation to North Vietnam visit a textile mill in Hanoi. Pham Van Dong, Premier of North Vietnam, is in the row behind Chou on the right.

Cartoons

IT'S TOUGH

By Ying Tao

We attract bullets just like a magnet!

How come our weapons work much better in their hands!

"Light casualties" is what the government said....

The USA is sitting on a volcano!

(From *Renmin F*

Chinese cartoons on the American situation in Vietnam.

In 1950 Chiang Kai-shek set up the Central Reform Committee for the restoration of 'China's territorial integrity'. The American and Kuomintang Mutual Defence Treaty of 1955, Article II, stated: 'In order more effectively to achieve the objective of this treaty, the parties separately and jointly by self-help and mutual aid will maintain and develop their individual and collective capacity to resist armed attack and Communist subversive activities directed from without against their territorial integrity and political stability.' (*China Handbook*, 1955–6)

PLA men training militia who are guarding an island on the Fukien front. (Taiwan is off the Fukien coast.)

'Washington put an embargo on China's trade . . . Her coastal navigation is still harassed by the US Seventh Fleet and Chiang's protected gunboats.' (Chen Yi, Chinese Foreign Minister, 1966)

One of the wrecked US pilotless reconnaissance military planes shot down by the Chinese PLA Air Force.

Sketch of U.S. Disposition for Aggression in Northeast Asia By Chu Yu-lien

PEOPLE'S REPUBLIC OF CHINA

Democratic People's Republic of Korea

JAPAN

Pacific

Ogasawara Islands (Japan)

Volcano Islands (Japan)

Okinawa (Japan)

Taiwan

U.S. imperialism is working against time to rig up its so-called "northeast Asia military alliance" consisting of Japan, south Korea and the Chiang Kai-shek gang. This is part of its vicious scheme of setting Asians to fighting Asians and of expanding its war of aggression in Asia.

Ocean

PHILIPPINES

Guam (U.S.A.)

✈ U.S. air base   ⚓ U.S. naval base   ⚙ U.S. missile site

Peking Union Medical College. 'To spend one million dollars to support colleges would have far greater political influence on the Chiang Kai-shek government than spending two millions on its army . . . an army might revolt, whereas students trained in American-run colleges would be obedient and reliable.' (*China Reconstructs*, 1968)

China in the United Nations. Britain supported her entry. On 24 September 1971, Reuter reported: 'Britain voted against the US proposal in the US steering committee. Sir Colin Crowe, the chief British delegate, said he had instructions to oppose any substantive resolution or procedural motion that would delay Peking's entry.' On the other hand, they reported, 'the US ambassador warned reporters this morning: "If they try to knock out our item we shall fight". The American proposal seeks dual representation. Under this both Peking and Taiwan would have UN membership but Peking would take the powerful Security Council seat now held by Chiang Kai-shek's Taiwan Government'. France supported China's admission.

English ping-pong players give an exhibition match for a workers' community in Shanghai.

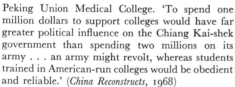

The meeting between Chairman Mao Tse-tung and President Richard Nixon of the United States, with, left, Chou En-lai who said: 'At the present time it has become a strong desire of the Chinese and American peoples to promote the normalisation of relations between the two countries and work for the relaxation of tension. The social systems of China and the United States are fundamentally different, and there exist great differences between the Chinese government and the United States government. However, these differences should not hinder China and the United States from establishing normal state relations on the basis of the Five Principles of mutual non-aggression, non-interference in each other's internal affairs, equality and mutual benefit, and mutual co-existence; still less should they lead to war . . .' In reply, President Nixon said: 'While we cannot close the gulf between us, we can try to bridge it so that we may be able to talk across it . . . There is no reason for us to be enemies.'

'The successful explosion of China's first hydrogen bomb on 17 June 1967 represents another leap in the development of China's nuclear weapons. At no time and in no circumstances will China be the first to use nuclear weapons.' (*Peking Review*)

Workers at the Peking No. 2 Steel Rolling Mill, in Tien Anmen Square, celebrating the successful launching of China's first man-made earth satellite.

Worker technicians in charge of the trial manufacture of China's first electron microscope with a magnification of 200 000 times.

Workers at the Shanghai Electrical Equipment Plant installing a generator.

'An unusual number of economic delegations is converging on China these days. . . . Agents of two West German companies interested in selling steel arrived lately and trade delegations from Yugoslavia and East Germany are expected soon. . . . Both the Japanese and the French are planning big trade shows in Peking.' (*Toronto Globe and Mail*, 1970) On display at China's Export Commodities Fair is a numerical control vertical six-spindle turret jig drilling and boring machine.

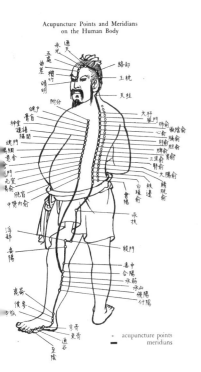

Acupuncture Points and Meridians
on the Human Body

· acupuncture points
— meridians

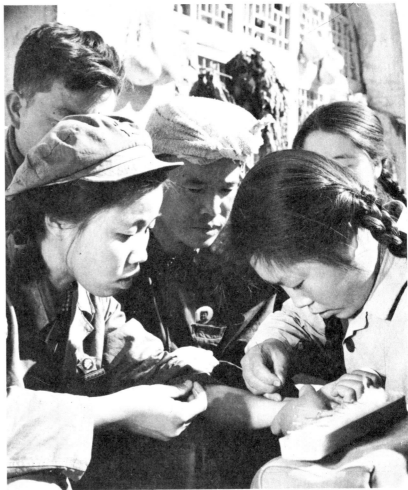

Ancient diagram of acupuncture points and meridians on the human body.

Medical teams giving training in acupuncture treatment to barefoot doctors. Dr E. Grey Dimond, Provost for Health Sciences at the University of Missouri, Kansas City, commented to the *American Medical News* on his return from China: 'I saw more of acupuncture than I know how to believe. As you stand there watching these proceedings your scientific brain says, "My God this can't be". But you're still standing there watching it. I'm sure I'm not sure how it works, but I have to believe there is some margin of truth in it.' Dr Dimond observed the removal of part of a lung and other lung operations.

Another participant in the co-operation between China and the West.

3 China and the West: 1793-1950

The East–West conflict opened in 1793 with the Emperor Chien Lung's historic 'no' to the request by Lord Macartney, on behalf of His Britannic Majesty George III, for trade and diplomatic exchanges. Increasing quantities of opium were sold to China by Britain (helped by venal court officials and greedy Chinese merchants), with disastrous effects on her health and economy. Between 1829 and 1839 China sent abroad as payment for opium some 100 million ounces of silver. Strongman Lin Tse-hsu destroyed some 20 000 chests of the drug in a sort of Boston tea-party. As a result the British, and later the French, landed with trained troops, whose strength the Chinese, totally unused to modern arms, at first failed to understand.

Commissioner Lin commented: 'With respect to British soldiers, they lack skill in using fists and swords like proper fighters. Also, their legs are firmly bound with cloth, and in consequence it is very inconvenient for them to stretch. . . . They can do little harm and therefore, what is called their power can be controlled without difficulty.'

Their power, of course, could not be controlled—certainly not by the hopelessly antiquated imperial forces. The Opium War, the first of many, had started. Destruction and suffering were widespread as armies burned and plundered and, later, European employers recruited cheap 'coolie' labour. Filled with a nice amalgam of religious and commercial fervour, many in the West saw themselves as bringing industrial and spiritual enlightenment to the 'heathen Chinee'. The *Illustrated London News* said unctuously in 1843: 'England has at this solemn hour to teach the Chinese to cast off superstition, break its fetters, and come down in humility to the religion of Christ.' But it is good to note that a vigorous protest movement by an Opium War moratorium lobby was widely supported by scholars, clergy and the general public in England. The influential magazine, the *Spectator*, wrote: 'There never was a civilised people who had suffered such a series of appalling insults. . . . The whole mandarin class has been penetrated with an abhorrence of foreigners from whom they have suffered such losses, such cruelties and above all such inexpiable insults.' Protests were unavailing, of course; the war went on and the defeated China signed the Treaty of Nanking by which more Chinese ports were opened up to European traders, the island of Hong Kong was ceded to Her Britannic Majesty, and a payment of some six million dollars was demanded for the destroyed opium.

From 1858 to 1860 Britain and France fought the Second Opium War, wringing still more commercial and territorial concessions from the hapless emperor; the indemnities caused a steady flow of silver from the national coffers, impoverishing millions and including, incidentally, some Europeans, for trade between England and China was checked. It was at the end of this war that Lord Elgin ordered and supervised the notorious burning of the vast and beautiful Summer Palace near Peking, with its priceless art treasures. (He said he was reluctant to do this but argued that he had to take drastic action against the Chinese since they had not honoured their agreements with him and had killed some European hostages.) From 1850 to 1865 the great peasant rebellion of the Taipings (Heavenly Kingdom of the Great Peace) racked China. Its agonies and destruction, in which millions died, were aggravated and protracted by Western mercenaries hired by the imperial official, Li Hung-chang, for a Court alarmed by the wide popular support for the basic social reforms demanded by the Taipings. French, British, American and a scattering of other European troops were recruited. Two foreign leaders earned fame—or notoriety: Frederick Ward, an American who was killed in action during the fighting, and the Englishman ,Major Charles George Gordon, widely romanticised as defender of the faith in China and later in the Sudan. To the Chinese Court and gentry Gordon was a stalwart ally; to the Chinese today, of course, he is another betrayer of the people's cause. An *Overland Trade Report* of 1862 commented critically: 'Since the death of Admiral Protet the French troops have been behaving like fiends, killing indiscriminately men, women and children. Truth demands the confession that British sailors have likewise been guilty of revolting barbarities, not only upon the Taipings, but on inoffensive, helpless country people. It is a most singular circumstance . . . that the Taipings have never yet committed an act of retaliation upon any European who may have fallen into their hands.'

The anti-Western bitterness generated in these years was aggravated by the growing number of Christian missionaries admitted, along with the gunboats by the Treaty of Tientsin in 1860. These became the target of bitter nationalist resentment as they demanded more privileges and more opportunities to proselytise. An imperial decree of 15 March 1899 giving special rights to French Catholic bishops was especially resented. Severe punishment for the murderers of several missionaries precipitated yet another rebellion—the Boxer—and yet another defeat for peasant and imperial soldiers alike. Eight foreign armies marched into and sacked Peking after lifting the famous fifty-five days' Boxer siege of the Legations.

The Emperor Wilhelm II, and Field-Marshall Count von Waldersee who led the German contingent, were probably not alone in their attitude to the Chinese. 'Just as the Huns a thousand years ago . . . gained a reputation by virtue of which they still live in historical tradition, so may the name of Germany become known in such a manner in China, that no Chinese will ever again dare to look askance at a German.'

It was now abundantly clear that the West's demands were insatiable and that China's humiliations would continue as long as the tragic inferiority of her corrupt, moribund, anachronistic government continued. Nation-wide soul-searching produced demands for reform; 'self-strengthening' movements sprang up everywhere, led, at first, by the intellectuals, who were the first to realise what was happening and to grasp the magnitude of the gap which yawned between the quality of their armies and those of the Western powers. Tan Ssu-tung, in a letter to Kang Yu-wei, said: 'Helplessly we have to purchase these things [arms] from foreign countries. But the foreigners know that China has no machinery to test the quality of weapons and no way to distinguish between good and bad, so they sell to China at an exorbitant price weapons which already have been abandoned . . . we should learn the written and spoken language of all countries so as to translate Western books and newspapers in order to know what other countries are doing all around us.'

The Chinese had to admit the military superiority of the Europeans, but aesthetically and socially the latter scarcely commanded Chinese respect with their large noses, hirsute chests and faces, their smoking habits and, surprisingly, their uxoriousness. Westerners seemed truly barbarians to the Chinese, but Western scorn for the Chinese was even greater, and every reader of *Punch* and the London press began to accept the still-familiar stereotypes of the 'chinks' as sly, slant-eyed, menacing figures of barely human creatures with odious oriental habits.

Chinese workers in foreign-owned factories received starvation wages for working long hours in bad conditions, and it was not long before the merchants and *petit bourgeoisie* realised that they, also, were suffering from Western exploitation and chicanery. They, too, joined the reform movement. 'In May 1904 the Shanghai Chamber of Commerce passed a resolution to the effect that if the US imperialists did not stop maltreating Chinese workers and overseas Chinese within two months it would launch a movement to boycott American goods. Meanwhile an anti-US movement began to unfold in various other places. When the two months' limit expired in July the US imperialists still insisted on signing a new treaty. The Chinese people were indignant and the anti-US movement was unprecedented in scale. With Shanghai as its centre it swept over the whole country.'

A sad example of Western sharp practice was the acquisition of the Kaiping Mines, the nucleus of the vast Kailan Mining administration. Herbert Hoover, later to become the President of the USA, was closely connected with the deal. The Chinese brought a case against him and his colleagues which was tried in London by Mr Justice Joyce, whose summing up made only too clear that Western chicanery had won a considerable financial victory over the Chinese.

Reform demands got nowhere and the Empress Dowager, looking resolutely backwards, transformed a reform movement into a revolutionary one. Its leader, Sun Yat-sen, educated in the West and with many friends there, turned to England and America for support but received little.

After several abortive and bloody attempts the revolutionaries, helped by defecting imperial troops, captured the great military city of Wuhan in 1911 and the imperial house crumbled with barely a further shot.

Over two thousand years of dynastic rule was ended.

Sun became President, but not with the approval of Western nations, suspicious of his 'Socialist' notions. They preferred to lend their support to his rival, Yuan Shih-kai, and later, to the various war-lords who marched and counter-marched across the wretched land. Japan, as well as the Western powers, supported one or other side in these civil conflicts, aggravating the national misery.

For China, the great betrayal came at the end of World War I, when the notorious Article 156 of the Treaty of Versailles took from the Germans their territories in China, only to hand them over to Japan. 'The territories around Kiaschow Bay, the cables and mines of Shantung and other privileges set forth in the German treaty of 1898 are to be ceded to Japan. Germany's rights and railroads, main lines and spurs, properties, stations, buildings . . . and mines are to be taken over by Japan. The cables from Tsingtao to Formosa are to be taken over unconditionally by Japan.'

When the Japanese took over Manchuria in 1931, another Western consortium, the League of Nations, failed to do more than make protesting noises at the League's Lytton Commission meetings. Japan's aggression at this time, and her subsequent occupation, until 1945, of other parts of China, went unchecked, compounding the suffering already inflicted by the West.

Many Western conservatives must have agreed with British Minister L. S. Amery when he expressed sympathy for the Japanese point of view; others shared Chinese concern about Western support —tacit or open—for Japan.

When China's Anti-Japanese War became the Allie's Anti-Japanese War after Pearl Harbour, President Roosevelt tried to initiate a policy of military co-operation with the Communist guerrillas in Northern China; General Stilwell, Commander-in-Chief of the US forces in the Far East, was enthusiastic, and so in 1944 the exploratory 'Mission to Yenan', comprising several experienced American diplomats, started negotiations with the Red armies. Stilwell approved but Chiang did not, and neither did the US Ambassador Patrick Hurley. In a 1971 TV documentary the four Americans, John Davies, John Service, Ray Ludden and John Emerson, recounted their experiences in this crucial mission.

Service: 'There was a great deal of friendship on both sides.'

Emerson: 'We found that the people were active, they were enthusiastic. Just talking to them gave you a certain amount of confidence when you heard about what they were doing. All of this contributed to an atmosphere, I think, which was a very favourable one, and probably even more favourable because of the contrast to what we had left behind in Chung-King. Those of us who had lived in Chung-King became very depressed because the political atmosphere was very depressing—one heard only stories of corruption, of deals one way and another; the Chinese were not really fighting the Japanese in the war.'

Ludden: 'The feeling between the Americans and the Chinese Communists in Yenan was very amicable indeed.'

Service: 'We arrived there in July, and we had all sorts of missions. We wanted to tap what intelligence they had about Japanese military forces, military strength, order of battle information. . . . We wanted to set up a weather-reporting network because they held strategic areas all over North China. The Fourteenth Air Force needed to have prognosis of the weather before they started bombing missions. . . . I don't think there's ever been such a period of cordiality between America and China. Certainly we had more forthgoing co-operation, with less demands, less conditions, up there than we had in Nationalist China at that time. Furthermore, I doubt if there's ever been a Communist society, or Communist régime, that laid itself so open. That rescued something like seventy American pilots and air crew all over North China; they allowed us to go anywhere. . . . The potentiality for guerrilla activity was just fantastic.'

Service: 'The policy of the American government at this time, really, was to avoid a complete commitment to Chiang Kai-shek, because it was quite obvious in the balance of forces in China, that the future of Chiang Kai-shek's government was in doubt. The Communists, from what we reported, and many people were reporting, had greater vitality, organisational power, support of the people, and so on. And we did not wish to commit ourselves wholly to the support of a party that was going to lose. But Hurley was a maverick loose in the range, and there was simply no way apparently of putting a rein on him.'

Incredibly, it was Chiang and the maverick that won the day. Stilwell was recalled, the report ignored and its authors discredited. John Service records the disasters that flowed from their defeat. (Emerson's comment, made at the time of President Nixon's Peking visit, is significant.)

Service: 'We would have maintained our relations—there never would have been a break. There wouldn't be an exile government in Taiwan; and probably there would not have been a Korean War. Very likely, if you follow things through, there might not have been a Vietnam War.'

Emerson: 'But I believe that what Mao is saying today is similar to what he was saying to us in 1944. So I do believe then that there is a great opportunity for us at the present time to again develop a relationship with the government of Mainland China.'

Victory over Japan brought no peace to China. Civil war followed. The Red armies fighting the Nationalist forces must have heard the echoes of the Taiping and Boxer Rebellions, for the United States gave massive military support in the form of ammunition and weapons to Chiang's side to prevent China 'going Red'.

'Would the US agree to the appointment of US officers to actual command of the China army units under the pretence of acting as advisers?' was the request by T. F. Tsing for the KMT in 1948. General Marshall saw the hopelessness of Chiang's cause and advised accordingly in a memorandum in November, 1948. 'It would be a very serious matter for the US to send an officer to almost certain failure,' he wrote.

When the defeated Chiang fled the mainland for the island of Taiwan, US support was to continue for many more years.

to your entreaty to send one of your nationals
be accredited to my Celestial Court and to be
control of your country's trade with China, this
uest is contrary to all usage of my dynasty and
not possibly be entertained. . . . Your merchants
assuredly never be permitted to land or reside
e. . . . Do not say you were not warned in due
e—tremblingly obey and show no negligence.
special mandate.' (The Chien Lung Emperor
King George III)

ter from a schoolboy, Master Stanhope, a
hew of a member of Lord Macartney's Embassy
793 describing the celebration of Chien Lung's
tieth birthday.

The Emperor Chien Lung in the Summer Palace, painting attributed to Giuseppe Castiglione (Lang Shih-ning) 1698–1766.

Commissioner Lin Tse-hsu.

Commissioner Lin Tse-hsu seized 20 882 chests opium and had them burnt: 'First I had a series trenches dug . . . and after this diverted water i the trenches. Then I had salt sprinkled on pools. Finally, I had the unprocessed opium fl into the pools and added lime to boil the opium it was turned into ashes and completely destroy The nauseating odour was more than we co bear.'

'The battleship *Nemesis* . . . set fire to the city of Shanghai which was occupied by our troops, its public buildings burned, its rich granaries, the property of the government given up to the people. An incessant cannonade was kept up for two hours ere the enemy showed any symptoms of submission.' (*Illustrated London News*, 1842)

'No language could convey a description of the sufferings of those to whom opium has become a necessary of existence; no picture could impress the fearful misery which the inmates of an opium smoking shop exhibit. These dens of human suffering are attended by unfortunate women—as opium in the early use is an aphrodisiac, and as such prized by the Chinese. Once fairly begun, there is no cessation until poverty and death ensue; the utmost effect of the drug is merely to mitigate the horrors of existence. The opium shops I visited were perfect types of hell on earth.' (*Chinese Politics, Commerce and Society*, by R.M. Martin)

During every hour of Queen Victoria's reign half a ton of opium was, on an average, exported from India. 'The spectacular increase in the opium trade during the first half of the nineteenth century is best illustrated by plain figures: 1817, 3210 chests (containing some 150 pounds each) of Indian opium. 1827, 9969 chests; 1833, nearly 24 000; 1837, 34 000; 1860, 85 000.' (*The Stranger in China*, by C. Toogood Downing) The Rev. Dr Moulton, the President of Wesleyan College, cried out: 'If the people of England could realise what is going on in China we should have something like a revolution—throughout the Christian churches at all events. It has been called "England's greatest contribution to the wretchedness of the world".'

Hong Kong soon after 1842, the year it was ceded to the British.

The Summer Palace, the day before its destruction.
(*Illustrated London News*, 1861)

The ruins of the Summer Palace. 'On the afternoon of the twenty-fourth vast columns of smoke were seen rising to the north-west, and it was ascertained that the barbarians had entered the Summer Palace and after plundering the three main halls, leaving them absolutely bare, they had set fire to the buildings. Their excuse for this abominable behaviour is that their troops got out of hand and had committed the incendiarism. After this they issued notices, placarded everywhere, in very bad Chinese, stating that unless terms of peace had been arranged before midday on the twenty-ninth, they would bombard Peking, in which case all the inhabitants who did not wish to share the fate of the city had better remove themselves to safe distance.' (*China Under the Empress Dowager*, by J. Bland and E. Backhouse)

The French spoils exhibited at the Tuileries included the Emperor's war costume, a seven-foot high pagoda, golden sceptres and daggers and porcelain. 'Their real value can never be estimated. A figure of 2 million pounds is suggested. The loot is disposed of according to the caprice of the victors. Thirty cases have been sent to Napoleon III, the Emperor of France. Promoted from the palatial abode of Emperor Hsien Fou to that of Napoleon III they have merely changed their address without compromising their dignity.' (*Illustrated London News*, 1861)

Li Hung-chang at the age of 74. The *Illustrated London News* reported that: 'Gordon collected a small but well-equipped force of native troops and trained them with European discipline near Soochow.' Li Hung-chang was no less flattering: 'It is a direct blessing from Heaven, I believe, the coming of the British Gordon. He is superior in manner and bearing to any of the foreigners I have come across and does not show outwardly that conceit which makes most of them repugnant in my sight. Besides which, he is direct and business-like; within two hours of his arrival he was inspecting the troops, and I could not but rejoice at the manner in which his commands were obeyed.'

'The Westerners particularly rely upon the excellence and efficacy of their guns, cannon, and steamships, and so they can overrun China. The bow and spear, small guns, and native-made cannon which have their bullets fed from the main opening, the sailing boats, rowboats, and gunboats which have been hitherto employed cannot oppose their steam-engined warships. Therefore, we are controlled by the Westerners.' (*Problems of Industrialisation*, by Li Hung-chang)

A Chinese Commander and a fusilier.

'Any comparison to the state of Chinese military preparedness was simply laughable. The guns of Shanhaiknan "were remnants of the early Ming which had to be overhauled for use". The Yangtze River, the so-called "natural barrier" of defence, had already been occupied by the British. Those who are in charge of military affairs are all literary officials . . . they have no knowledge of armaments.' (Governor of Chihli)

'...ing the Chinese Melon'

'...e Russians are spying on us in the North, and ...English peeping at us on the West; the French ...staring at us in the South, the Japanese are ...hing us in the East. Living in the midst of ...e four strong neighbours, and being the Middle ...gdom, China is in imminent peril.' (Kang ...vei, 1895)

...avant!' Russia (aside): 'I do hope his motives ...as disinterested as mine.' The beginning of ...ry between Japan and Russia.

...ese: 'Now I have a gun I'll fight.'
...opean: 'I only want to trade.'
...ese: 'We have a Ministry of Commerce and a ...inistry of Foreign Affairs.'
...opean: 'Do they protect your interests or ours?'

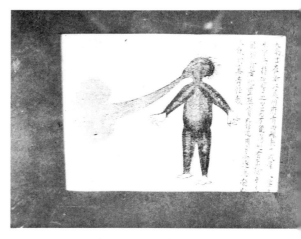

Chinese caricature of a British sailor.

A CHANSON FOR CANTON.

JOHN CHINAMAN a rogue is born,
The laws of truth he holds in scorn;
About as great a brute as can
Encumber the Earth is JOHN CHINAMAN.
  Sing YEH, my cruel JOHN CHINAMAN,
  Sing Yeo, my stubborn JOHN CHINAMAN;
  Not COBDEN himself can take off the ban
  By humanity laid on JOHN CHINAMAN.

With their little pig-eyes and their large pig-tails,
And their diet of rats, dogs, slugs, and snails,
All seems to be game in the frying-pan
Of that nasty feeder, JOHN CHINAMAN.
  Sing lie-tea, my sly JOHN CHINAMAN,
  No fightee, my coward JOHN CHINAMAN:
  JOHN BULL has a chance—let him, if he can,
  Somewhat open the eyes of JOHN CHINAMAN.

19. 'A Chanson for Canton'. A heathen Chinee against a willow-pattern background. This verse and cartoon which appeared in *Punch* on 10 April 1858, concisely reflects popular conceptions of China at the time.

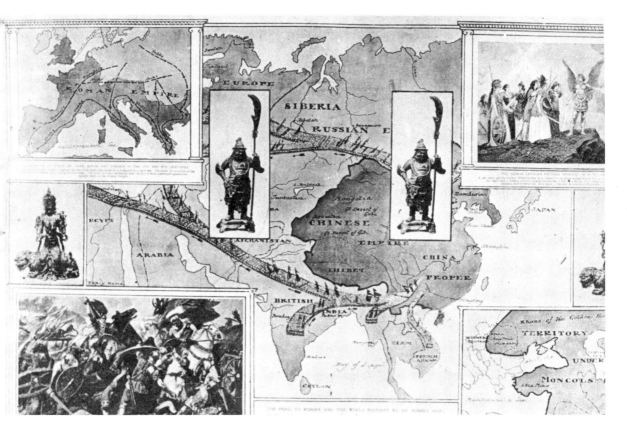

'Sir Robert Hart . . . forsees in China dangers which "will imperil the world's future". These words will doubtless provoke a laugh. Well, let them do so but let them stand. 20 000 000 or more of Boxers, armed, drilled, disciplined and animated by patriotic if mistaken motives will make residence in China impossible for foreigners—will take back from foreigners everything that foreigners have taken from China and will pay off old grudges with interest.' (*China's Past and Future*, by A. Holcombe and B. Broomhall)

A party of English missionaries who went to China in the early part of this century.

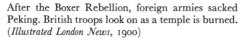

After the Boxer Rebellion, foreign armies sacked Peking. British troops look on as a temple is burned. (*Illustrated London News*, 1900)

United States marines march into Peking—Boxer Rebellion. (*Illustrated London News*, 1900)

Legation hospital during the siege of Peking. (*Illustrated London News*, 1900)

'The Christian religion inculcates the practise of virtue . . . persons teaching it or possessing it shall be entitled to the protection of the Chinese authorities. . . . British warships shall be at liberty to visit all ports.' (Treaty of Tientsin) Chinese Christians under escort after the siege of Peking.

Shooting the Manchus.

Victory, 1911.

The Kailan Mining Administration building. 'The promoters, as I understand, distributed the shares and allotted the debentures among themselves and their friends, who still have, I suppose, the 424 993 fully paid up shares for which nothing has, in fact, been paid.' (Mr Justice Joyce, *The Times*, 2 March 1905)

Kailan Mining Administration.

Perspective of New Head Offices.

Chiang Kai-shek

Yuan Shih-kai. *The Times* described him as 'the only man who can prevent the Chinese Republic from falling to pieces'.

'The Doormat.' (Cartoon by David Low) 'Who is to say that Japan ought not to have acted as she did with the object of defending herself . . . against a vigorous Chinese nationalism. Our whole policy in India and in Egypt stands condemned if we condemn Japan . . . it would be no concern of ours if such a quarrel [between the USSR and Japan] developed into a war to prevent Japanese expansion in Eastern Siberia.' (L. S. Amery)

Chinese war graves in France.

Public executions by Chinese war-lords. 'In the ten years between 1917 and 1927, when Chiang Kai-shek came to power, more than fifteen hundred military chieftans, war-lords big and small, devastated the land . . . each in turn shot to prominence as the future "strong man" in the press, of which every Western country was paying and supplying him with the extra ammunition and guns left over from the First World War of Europe.' (*The Crippled Tree*, by Han Suyin)

US warships in Shanghai Harbour during the 1930s.

Mao Tse-tung and Chou En-lai.

Kuomintang troops being transported to the north-east civil war front by US army planes after the Chungking peace agreement was signed. 'It was perfectly clear to us that if we told the Japanese [in 1945] to lay down their arms immediately and march to the seaboard the entire country would be taken over by the Communists. We therefore had to take the step of using the enemy as a garrison until we could airlift Chinese National troops to North China. So the Japanese were instructed to hold their places and maintain order. In due course Chinese troops under Chiang Kai-shek would appear, the Japanese would surrender to them, march to the seaports, and we would send them back to Japan.' (*President Truman's Memoirs*, vol. II, 1956)

The signing of treaties at the United Nations.
—Russia—modern—

China and Russia

'Hand in glove with Western Imperialist countries tsarist Russia compelled China to sign a number of unequal treaties after the Opium War, 1840.' (Modern Communist historian)

'Kruschev suggested that Moscow and Peking should "synchronise their watches". There are two watches; which is to be the master watch?' (Peking Review, 1963)

4 China and Russia

Although imperial Russia was one of the first two European powers to come into contact with Manchu-ruled China in the mid-seventeenth century, Russia's influence was the least of all the foreign nations' until it became the greatest in the twentieth century. Although some roots of Chinese Communism lay in the original Communist doctrines of Western Europe, its main inspiration came from the Russian Revolution of 1917, and for several years the small Chinese Communist Party was under direct Russian Communist control and indirect leadership. Mao Tse-tung's movement in the interior of South China broke this too-close link, and the Chinese party then developed, in virtual isolation, its own style, its native leadership and its considerable independence of Russian practice, if not avowedly of theory also. During the years following the Communist Party's victory in China in 1949 and 1956, Russia was the admitted model, the only real friend and the sole ally of the Chinese People's Republic. But after the death of Stalin and the denunciation of his policies by Kruschev in 1956, China drew away from the Soviet, and what was at first an ideological difference steadily widened into an acrimonious dispute, which also embraced national interests and questions of territorial claims, especially along the Amur River border. This dispute, even though it is not quite so vigorously pursued in polemical debate today, remains the underlying influence determining the relations between the two countries, not only in the political field, but equally in that of ideology.

Today, the influence of Russia in China is slight, or negative; the USSR is not a model to be copied but a warning of something to be avoided. Revisionism, a dilution of the true revolutionary doctrine, a willingness to compromise not only with foreign 'imperialists' but with *bourgeois* trends within society, is the failing which China sees in her erstwhile ally and exemplar. This leads to the claim, unacceptable to the Russian leadership, that China, and above all Mao himself, is the true model for revolutionary Communism; the only progressive road to follow is the path indicated by the Thought of Mao Tsetung. In certain aspects the rejection of Russia today matches the indifference and aversion to imperial Russia shown by the reformers and revolutionaries who sought to modernise China fifty years ago. Russia, then an empire ruled by an autocrat, exhibited few features attractive to Chinese reformers, who were themselves bent on altering their own, similar, political system. Russian literary culture, which was always tinged with revolutionary thinking, was seen as one aspect of Western culture rather than as something specifically Russian. Few Chinese could read Russian; the works they knew were English translations of the great Russian writers.

On the other hand, the educated Chinese were well aware that imperial Russia was a bad neighbour and a potential menace. From being remote in the seventeenth and eighteenth centuries, and only marginal in the nineteenth century, the Russian threat became real with the construction of the Trans-Siberian Railway and the Russian occupation of that region of Central Asia west of China's outlying dominion of Sinkiang. Russia was a land power; her pressure was exerted upon the frontiers of the empire, and finally within them, in Manchuria. As Russia was not a model to be copied, she remained simply a menace to be feared. Russian encroachment in the 1860s in what is now Eastern Siberia (then an outlying tributary tribal territory of the Manchu Empire) and in the 1880s along the western frontier of Sinkiang, portended what might come later. In the twentieth century, as a result of the opportunity provided by the Boxer Rebellion, Russia moved into Manchuria, only to be ejected from the southern half of that huge territory by Japan in 1905. But Russia remained in the north; Harbin, like Port Arthur (Lushun), a Russian-built city, had a very large Russian population which treated the country more like an annexed colony than a foreign land.

The Russian Revolution produced a dramatic change. The danger of Russia seemed to disappear. The new Russia, professing equality of all peoples, abandoned the privileges of the tsarist régime (but not the territory which the tsars had taken) and became the most interesting country to the Chinese educated class of the early republic, a class thoroughly disillusioned by the course which their own revolution had taken. Marxist literature and Leninist doctrine were soon familiar to the educated Chinese of the younger generation, several years before a Chinese Communist Party existed. The Russian Revolution was not seen with the horror that it caused in Europe; the execution of a fallen imperial family had been the normal fate of the defeated in China, and the Manchu imperial house was deemed very fortunate to have escaped it by a timely abdication. The overthrow of a privileged nobility was positively admired in China. The renunciation of imperialist privileges and claims, even if this was perhaps not so thorough as it professed to be, stood out in stark contrast to the actions and policies of the Western powers and Japan. The stage was set for a great surge of Russian influence born on the impetus of Communist revolution.

Communism was a Western economic and political doctrine which the West had rejected for this very reason; it seemed to many educated Chinese to offer the advantages of a modern—the most modern—revolutionary doctrine and programme for economic development without the disagreeable consequences of being bound to the Western capitalist economic system, which to the Chinese meant foreign exploitation. Russia had outleapt the West, and China should take her as the new model. And yet, here too the inherent selectiveness of Chinese response to foreign influences was also manifest. Before very long the Chinese Communists were making their own policies, relying on social factors which the Russians did not take into account, and rejecting, at first implicitly, later explicitly, some of the main doctrines of Russian revolutionary thinking. A Russian diplomat of great experience and long-standing knowledge of China remarked to an Australian colleague in 1948: 'Yes, we are making the running; but the Chinese will use us, as they used you, and cast us off, as they have cast you off.' It would be interesting to know if he reported in these terms to his government, at that time presided over by Stalin.

Today, China has a difficult and ambivalent relationship with the region closest to her and bound to her by the oldest ties of contact—South East Asia. The newly independent nations, and Thailand—the only one never to fall under colonial rule—are strongly nationalist, and in many of them dwell large Chinese communities who are envied and sometimes discriminated against on grounds of race and alleged economic domination. In some of these countries there have been, and perhaps again soon will be, open Communist-led revolts which make China their model and seek the violent overthrow of their governments. China is therefore under suspicion, not always necessarily correct, of inspiring such movements. On the other hand, trade with China is of growing importance to all the countries in this area, and they cannot prosper if they persecute too severely the Chinese commercial and business class, who in practice direct and control much of the economy. Chinese policy since the People's Republic has veered between support for revolution on ideological grounds, as in Vietnam, and restraint upon revolutionary activity for fear of reprisals on and harsh treatment of the Chinese community, as in Indonesia and also Malaysia. The region is, has been historically, and will in future inevitably be overshadowed by the power of a strong China. The nations of South-east Asia will have to live with China, long after the US presence has followed the colonial empires into the past. But at the present time there are serious tensions and potential dangers in the relations between China and South-east Asia.

Since the greater part of the region was under European colonial rule in the nineteenth century, the impact of South-east Asia upon China has not been important until very recent times. Western influences reached China by more direct routes; the educational level of the Chinese in South-east Asia was below that of the educated class in China for a long time and such influence as was exerted tended to come from China, rather than affecting China herself. In the more distant past, South-east Asia was one of the routes by which Buddhism, and later Islam, reached China, but these foreign cultural influences are now of only historical interest. In spite of a very long period of contact, often continuous and close, neither China nor the South-east Asian lands greatly influenced each other in culture or in art. One reason was the diversity of languages and scripts used in South-east Asia; another was the fact that the Chinese language and literature did not touch the culture of the south beyond Vietnam. The cultural pattern which colonial rule left upon the nations of South-east Asia remains largely intact; Western languages are studied and spoken, but not those of their neighbours, nor Chinese, although Chinese form large minority groups in almost all these countries. The Chinese residents may learn the local language for business reasons, but their cultural allegiance remains strongly oriented towards China.

5 The People's Republic and the Soviet Union Today

Relations between the People's Republic of China and the Union of Soviet Socialist Republics are formal state-to-state relations, a different concept from relations between the Communist Party of the Soviet Union (CPSU) and the Chinese Communist Party (CCP).

From 1917 to 1949 Moscow maintained state-to-state relations with the Nationalist government in Nanking or Chungking and the Soviet ambassador was with Chiang Kai-shek's government until the very moment of the flight to Taiwan.

At its inception the CCP saw itself as in tutelage to the CPSU. Although a master-disciple relationship, it was always uneasy, right up to the 1960s when the full extent of the Sino-Soviet split was clearly revealed as unbridgeable—even wider than that which existed between China and her old antagonist the USA.

From the start there were national, economic, cultural and, above all, doctrinal differences between Russia and China which have been aggravated rather than diminished by China's rise to power. In typically forthright fashion, Mao summed up the situation in an interview with the late Edgar Snow in 1971: 'As for ideology, who had fired the first shot? The Russians had called the Chinese dogmatists and then the Chinese had called them revisionists. China had published their criticisms, but the Russians had not dared publish China's. Then they had sent some Cubans, and later Rumanians, to ask the Chinese to cease open polemics. That would not do, Mao said. The polemics would have to be carried on for ten thousand years if necessary. Then Kosygin himself had come. After their talk Mao had told him that he would take off a thousand years but no more.

'The Russians looked down on the Chinese and also looked down on the people of many countries, he said; they thought that they had only to speak the word and all people would listen and obey. They did not believe that there were people who would not do so and that one of them was his humble self. Although Sino-Russian ideological differences were now irreconcilable they could eventually settle their problems as between states.'[1]

An account of post-1949 Sino-Soviet relations can most neatly start with Mao's first visit to Moscow on 16 December 1949. A Sino-Soviet Treaty, and two Sino-Soviet Agreements were signed by Mao and Stalin, including the Treaty of Friendship and Mutual Alliance Assistance, guaranteeing that 'if either country is attacked by Japan or any state allied with it, the other would immediately render military and other assistance by any means at its disposal'. In his farewell speech Mao said: 'The solidarity between the Soviet and Chinese peoples will be everlasting, indestructible and in-alienable.'

During the early 1950s warm people-to-people relations were established; Chinese children learned Russian, millions of copies of Soviet books were on sale. Many Chinese postage stamps bore Russian themes and there was a warm welcome for technicians and engineers in the farms and factories which Russian aid was helping to develop. This writer, for example, was told that great distress was felt in Wuhan steel mills when the Russian advisers were summarily recalled by Kruschev in 1960. Klaus Mehrhert describes listening to some young Chinese singing a song of friendship on the lake of the Summer Palace; the first two verses of their song were in Chinese, the third in Russian.

For a few years following 1949 Russia relinquished the various rights and privileges wrested from China by tsarist imperialism in the nineteenth century. The final renunciation came with Kruschev's Peking visit in 1954 when he and Bulganin paid generous tribute to the Chinese and signed agreements for financial and technical aid.* Soon after this Kruschev took the world by surprise with his anti-Stalin speech. The CCP was not amused, though the extent of its disapproval was not immediately evident, and Mao returned Kruschev's visit in 1957. 'The Socialist camp must have a head and this head is the USSR. The Communist parties of all countries must have a head and this head is the CPSU', said Mao. But his prophecy that 'the East wind would prevail over the West wind' may have sounded an independent note not wholly pleasing to his hosts, nor may his behind-the-scenes comments. 'Where necessary Mao waged struggle against them in order to correct their errors', wrote the Chinese press. But unity was at that time maintained, as the Chinese insisted a few years later.

By 1958, as has since been revealed in a torrent of accusation and counter-accusation between Moscow and Peking, the breach was steadily widening. The main divisive issues were Kruschev's adverse criticism of the communes and their function; the USSR's reneging on its agreement to share atomic know-how; Kruschev's signing of a non-proliferation agreement with Eisenhower, which left the Chinese —as they saw it—out in the cold war; Kruschev's ambivalent attitude on the first Sino-Indian border clashes and on China's armed clash with the Chinese nationalists over the Quemoy-Matsu islands in the Taiwan Straits in 1958; the steadily diminishing economic and technical aid from the USSR, and the periodic recrudescences of old-style Russian border incursions (denied by Russia).

To the Chinese such attitudes and actions were not only anti-China but anti-Marx, anti-Lenin and heretical; to use official terminology, they were proof of 'revisionism and social imperialism, [a] betrayal of the Revolution'. All Russian misdeeds flow from this basic treason.

The style and content of characteristic Chinese charges against the Soviet are illustrated in the Chinese response to a Tass statement of 1959, on the subject of the Sino-Indian border. Tass said: 'One cannot help regretting that an incident has occurred on the Sino-Indian frontier. The Soviet Union has friendly relations with the CPR as well as with the Republic of India. The Chinese and Soviet people are bound to one another by indissoluble friendship and co-operation between the Soviet Union and India is developing amicably. In leading Soviet circles the belief is expressed that both governments will eliminate misunderstanding in consideration of their mutual interests and in the spirit of the traditional friendship between the people of China and India.'

The Chinese put their point of view in strong terms: 'The internal differences were first brought into the open on 9 September 1959, to

* It is important to note that Russian aid, though invaluable at the time, was not as great as that given to other needy countries by the USSR. By 1957 Eastern Europe had been given 20 million roubles in credits and gifts; India 3·2 million; Iraq 730 million; and China 1·72 million. The total given by the USSR to non-Communist countries between 1954 and 1960 was roughly five times as much as China received from 1949 to 1960. These figures were quoted by Klaus Mehrhert in his book *Peking and Moscow*.

be exact. On that day a Socialist country turned a deaf ear to China's repeated explanations of the true situation and issued hastily a statement on the Sino-Indian border incident. Making no distinction between right and wrong they condemned the Chinese correct stand. Here is the first instance in history that a Socialist country, instead of condemning the provocation of the reactionaries of a capitalist country (India), condemned another fraternal Socialist country when it was confronted by armed provocation.'

There were other differences. The *Peking Review* said in 1959: 'The People's Communes represent the best organisational form for the gradual transition from Socialism to Communism; it will become the basic unit of the future Communist society.' But Kruschev commented from Poland: 'Those who wish to set up the communes have poor understanding of what Communism is and how it is to be built.'

The whole complex of doctrinal differences and the stresses they generated which led to the final declaration of Chinese independence are exhaustively set out, *inter alia*, in the series of letters exchanged between the protagonists in 1963.

The Chinese epitomised the doctrine developed during the years of the Chinese revolutionary struggle in *The Proposal Concerning the General Line of the International Communist Movement*. Subsequent correspondence from both sides was dealt with in *The Origin and Development of the Differences between the CPSU and Ourselves* in 1963. 'How have the differences arisen and how have they grown to their present dimensions?' asked the Chinese. 'There is a saying "it takes more than one cold day to freeze the river three feet deep". The present difficulties in the international Communist movement did not, of course, begin just yesterday—but seven years ago. To be specific it began with the twentieth congress of the CPSU in 1956. From the very outset we held that a number of views advanced at the twentieth congress were wrong; were violations of Marxism-Leninism. In particular the complete negation of Stalin—and the peaceful transition to Socialism by "the parliamentary road"—are gross errors of principle . . . Kruschev, . . . back from the Camp David talks, went so far as to try to sell China the US plot of the "two Chinas" . . . and read China a lecture against "tackling by force the stability of the capitalist system".' The record goes on: 'In June 1959 the Soviet government unilaterally tore up the agreement on new technology for national defence between the Soviet Union and China and refused to provide China with a sample of an atomic bomb and technical data concerning its manufacture.'

In 1965 the Central Committee of the CPSU accused China of actually seeking to foment a confrontation between the USSR and USA: 'On 29 September 1965 Chen Yi, Foreign Minister, spoke utterly falsely of a possible co-ordination of Soviet actions in North China with the aggressive war of the USA against the CPR. They want a clash of the USSR and the USA so that they may, as they say themselves, "sit on the mountain and watch the fight of the tigers".' Peking's *tu quoque* pulled no punches. The Central Committee of the CCP said in 1966: 'The leadership of the CPSU has become the centre of modern revisionism. You have intensified your activities against China . . . You have worked inside and outside the United Nations in a whole series of dirty deals with the USA. We would explicitly inform you that since you have gone so far the Communist Party of China, as a serious Leninist party, cannot send a delegation to this congress of yours.' The verbal clashes continued. Mao called Kruschev 'a buffoon on the contemporary historical stage propagating "phony communism"'.

In 1969 a serious armed clash occurred when forces from both sides faced each other on the ice-bound frontier of the far North-east Ussuri River region. Two simultaneous statements were issued about the Ussuri River clash. Peking: 'Russian gangsters helped by more than ten or twenty tanks and armoured cars came over the Ussuri River at 4 a.m. on 15 March.' Moscow: 'A big armed Chinese detachment supported by artillery and mortar fire today invaded Eastern Soviet territory and was repulsed.'

Peking insists that Chenpao Island has always been Chinese territory. The Russians, however, say that the lands beyond the Amur and the present maritime province of Siberia were not part of the Chinese state proper but were what might be termed the extramural possessions of the Manchu emperors who distinguished between their territory and that of China proper, that is, the Empire of the Ming which they acquired in 1644. Since these territories, like those on the Sinkiang border, are very remote and virtually closed to all foreign correspondents, the border arguments hardly admit of disinterested observations.

Professor Owen Lattimore commented that there seemed to be no real *casus belli* over which reason would not prevail, and Tilmon Durdin of the *New York Times* added that so far China had never laid formal claim to any 'unequal treaty' territories in this northern area. Fiery words were exchanged but, as ever, subsequent Chinese actions were reasonable. In 1969 they stated: 'We were ready to begin border negotiations. The Soviet people are not responsible [for Soviet policy] and considering that the working masses have been living in these territories for a considerable time the Chinese government is always disposed to take these unequal treaties as a basis for establishing a new alignment of boundaries between the two countries.' But China still keeps large numbers of frontier guards along all Sino-Soviet borders.

Once in the United Nations, the Chinese delegate carried war into the Soviet camp at the plenary session of that body on 26 November 1971: 'The partial nuclear test ban treaty and the treaty on nonproliferation of nuclear weapons jointly devised by the United States and the Soviet Union are something entirely imposed on others; they are aimed at monopolising nuclear weapons and controlling other countries. We can never agree to them. The Soviet leadership has carried out aggression, subversion, control and interference against other countries. This is clearly known to the representatives of many countries present here. China had her own experience in this respect . . . Countless facts have shown that what the Soviet leadership is practising is certainly not Socialism in words, [but] imperialism in deeds, that is, social-imperialism.'

In the early 1960s a new divisive element began to appear: Russia's perceptively friendly overtures to Taipei. In April 1972 the *New China News* published a bitter tirade: 'Showing interest in the recent plenary session of the Central Committee of the Kuomintang reactionaries, the *Soviet Weekly Times* had the audacity to call them "the ruling party in Taiwan" and Chiang Kai-shek "Generalissimo" and "Director-General" who was "nominated" as "President of the Republic of China" for a new term. With ulterior motives the journal even quoted from a Western news agency report the chants of "Long Live the Director-General" in hailing Chiang Kai-shek.

'This reveals fresh evidence of the crimes of the Soviet revisionist renegade clique which is stepping up its flirtation and collusion with the Chiang Kai-shek clique overthrown by the Chinese people long ago.'

At the same time the northern situation produced sporadic and alarmingly tense situations. In June 1972 *Washington Post* columnist, Jack Anderson, reported that President Nixon, in Moscow, had found his hosts 'obsessed' with Chinese leaders who, they claimed, 'had aspirations in India, Pakistan and Thailand'. Chinese leaders, in turn, confided to Henry Kissinger their fears about the Russians' extensive war preparations along the Mongolian border. The Chinese were moving crack troops to this area. Anderson commented on Washington's fears of a very serious military clash about which it was 'deeply disturbed'.

Perhaps what most angers the Soviet Union is China's claim to be the true doctrinal light; it is the East that is Red, and it is to China that the oppressed peoples of the neo-colonialist world most look for leadership. In March 1963 the *Peking Review* rejected the 'absurd' theory that Europe was the centre of the world and pointed out that 'the great victory of the Chinese revolution has a widespread influence in Asia, Africa and Latin America'. Earlier, a speech commemorating the founding of the Chinese Communist Party in 1951 stated that 'Mao Tse-tung's great accomplishment has been to change Marxism from a European to an Asiatic form'.

Sketch map showing intrusion by Soviets into the Chinese territory of Chenpao Island. 'On 2 March the Soviet revisionist clique sent armed soldiers to flagrantly intrude into Chenpao Island on the Wusuli River, Heilungkiang Province, and killed and wounded many frontier guards. This is an extremely grave armed border provocation, a frantic anti-China incident. The Soviet revisionist renegade clique shamelessly described Chen[...] Island as its territory alleging that Chinese gu[...] "crossed the Soviet state frontier". This is s[...] nonsense. It is an indisputable iron-clad fact [...] Chenpao Island, is Chinese territory. Lenin poi[...] out in 1900: "The policy of the Tsarist governm[...] is a criminal policy".' (*Down with the New T[...]* F.L.P.)

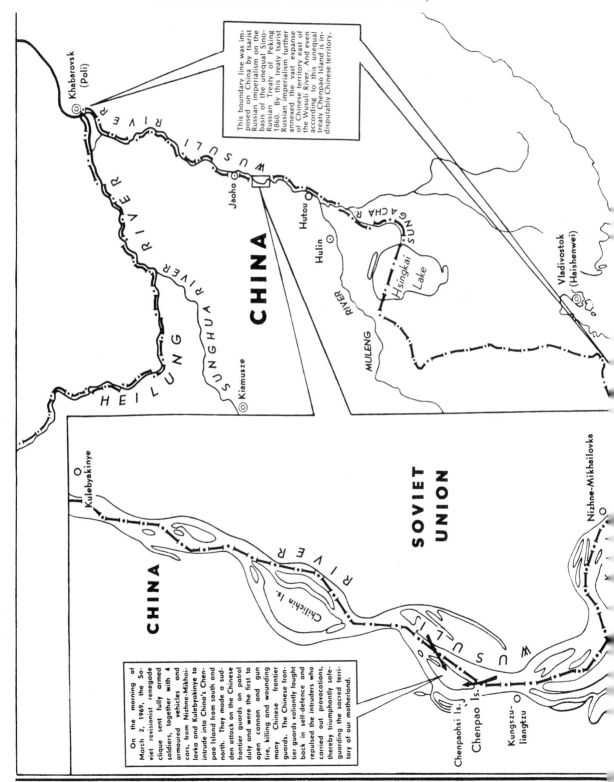

This boundary line was imposed on China by tsarist Russian imperialism on the basis of the unequal Sino-Russian Treaty of Peking 1860. By this treaty tsarist Russian imperialism further annexed the vast expanse of Chinese territory east of the Wusuli River. And even according to this unequal treaty Chenpao Island is indisputably Chinese territory.

On the morning of March 2, 1969, the Soviet revisionist renegade clique sent fully armed soldiers, together with 4 armoured vehicles and cars, from Nizhne-Mikhailovka and Kulebyakinye to intrude into China's Chenpao Island from south and north. They made a sudden attack on the Chinese frontier guards on patrol duty and were the first to open cannon and gun fire, killing and wounding many Chinese frontier guards. The Chinese frontier guards valiantly fought back in self-defence and repulsed the intruders who carried out provocations, thereby triumphantly safeguarding the sacred territory of our motherland.

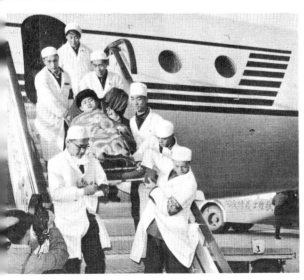

Mao Tse-tung, Bulganin and Stalin. On 16 December 1949 Mao Tse-tung visited the Soviet Union, an important event in the diplomatic history of the two countries. In his farewell, Mao said: 'The solidarity between the Soviet and Chinese peoples will be everlasting, indestructible and inalienable.'

Mao Tse-tung and Kruschev. 'After the Great October Revolution the victory of the Chinese people's revolution is the most outstanding event in world history with immense significance for the peoples of Asia. USSR and PRC are the invulnerable bastion of the camp of peace, democracy and socialism.' (Kruschev)

A Chinese student who was amongst those injured by Soviet soldiers, policemen and plain-clothes men returns to Peking. 'On 25 January 1967, some Chinese students while stopping over in Moscow on their way home from Europe . . . went to lay wreaths at Lenin's Mausoleum and Stalin's tomb to express their respect. Standing before Lenin's Mausoleum they read aloud two quotations from Chairman Mao. The students expressed the sincerest revolutionary regard of the Chinese people for the great Soviet people. Suddenly some 300 Soviet soldiers, policemen and plain-clothes men swarmed in and savagely attacked them, striking with their fists and kicking. Over 30 Chinese students were injured, four of them seriously.' (*China Pictorial*)

Chinese fishermen killed by Soviet armoured c

The frontier guards of a Chinese People's Libe
tion Army unit in Sinkiang discussing Mao Tset
Thought with local herdsmen.

On National Day, May Day and all major celebrations the portraits of Marx, Engels, Lenin and Stalin stand side by side in the great Tien Anmen Square with those of Sun Yat-sen and Mao Tsetung. They are also hung in public buildings. Here, delegates enter the meeting hall of the Party's ninth National Congress.

6 Imperial and Republican China: Imperial and Soviet Russia

When the Ussuri River clash occurred in 1969, Peking issued a booklet, *Down with the New Tsars*, which summarised the troubled Sino-Russian and Sino-Soviet relations in that area over the past two centuries, and implied that the present incidents were only too clearly the same mixture as before. For a better understanding of the contemporary scene it will be helpful to look at the circumstances in which these treaties were signed. We must remember that the hopeful, early distinction between imperial Russia and the USSR made by the People's Republic was to be briskly eroded, and that the Chinese came to see, in Kruschev and Kosygin, only Nicholas and Ivan all over again.

At the end of the nineteenth century a tsarist minister, Sergei Witte, voiced Russia's 'reasonable expectations in Asia', calmly stating that 'the absorption by Russia of a considerable proportion of the Chinese Empire is only a matter of time'.

Barely a decade later, another Russian minister commented: 'Our sovereign has grandiose plans in his head; he wants to seize Manchuria and proceed towards the annexation of Korea; he also plans to take Tibet under his rule.'

Ironically, Britain, one of Russia's rivals for Asian plunder, provided the opportunity for some of the Tsar's most successful claims on Chinese territory, when British and French wars in the south diverted the attention of the Manchus from Russia in the north. The *New York Daily Tribune* said, on 15 October 1858: 'It is by no means a comfortable reflection for John Bull that he himself by his first opium war, procured Russia a treaty yielding her the navigation of the Amur ... while the second opium war has helped her to the invaluable tract lying between the Gulf of Tartary and Lake Baikal, a region so much coveted by Russia ... that she has always attempted to get it.'

China's common borders with Russia stretch for some five thousand miles, a most contentious one being the Russo-Sinkiang border in the north-west of China. Frightened by Russian threats, China had to make many concessions. The region of Ili in that area was handed over to Russia by boundary agreements in the Treaty of St Petersburg, 1881, when part of the Kashgar and Kobdo districts were also lost. In addition, Russia was granted generous trading rights in Sinkiang and Mongolia, and as a bounty received an indemnity of some nine million roubles.

The Manchu Court, entrenched in the anachronistic fastnesses of the Forbidden City, nourished illusions of peaceful co-existence with the predators. A high official, Chang Chih-tung, advised the Emperor in 1895: 'To save the critical situation today, nothing is better than the conclusion of a secret treaty of alliance with a strong power for assistance.'

The suggestion was accepted, and while he was in Moscow in 1896 to attend the coronation of Nicholas II, Li Hung-chang signed a secret treaty very much in Russia's favour. As far as Russia was concerned, the land she had gained was of little use without communications, ports and trading posts, so she demanded, and was given, the right to build the Trans-Manchurian Railway to Vladivostok as a link in her Trans-Siberian line. Vladivostok (Haishenwei) had been assumed in 1860 more or less without a by-your-leave, and Port Arthur was wheedled out of the Emperor by a Russian dignitary who claimed to have negotiated the rescue of the Liaotung Peninsula from European powers. 'Never was a fine dominion so cheaply or more cleverly won', said England's Lord Curzon at the time.*

Many 'Russian' towns began springing up on Chinese soil. A French military mission visiting Manchuria was much impressed by the Russification of Port Arthur (now Lushan).

Marx and Lenin saw more clearly than the Manchu Court what was the aim of Russia and the Western powers—to partition China and share the spoils between them. Sun Yat-sen commented bitterly: 'All of this territory China gave over with folded hands to the foreigner without so much as a question.'

For China the Russian Revolution of 1917 not only eased the relentless pressure of imperialist expansion but also promised the restitution of territorial and commercial plunder of the past. The change was dramatically presented by the Karakhan Declaration and Manifesto in 1919–20: 'The Soviet government renounces all the seizures of Chinese territory and all Russian concessions in China without any compensation and forever, all that had predatorily been seized from her by the Tsarist government and the Russian *bourgeoisie*.'[1]

Less dramatic but more profound than these territorial renunciations, was the appeal of Marxist-Leninist thought and Russian revolutionary achievements on young Chinese patriots. Sun Yat-sen, inspired by Western democratic concepts, for years expected full European and American support for the infant Chinese republic which exploded into being early in the morning of 10 October 1911 with the fall of the Wuhan fortress to the revolutionaries. Denied this—'No sun rises in the West for China'—he turned to the Soviets.

In its national as well as doctrinal interests, Moscow sent financial help and political and administrative guidance through a series of advisers, the best-known being Michael Borodin and Adolf Joffe. In his last letter to the CPSU, shortly before his death, Sun recorded his high hopes for friendship between his country and Russia: 'You are at the head of the union of free republics—the heritage left to the oppressed peoples of the world by the immortal Lenin. . . . I leave behind me a Party, which, as I always hoped, would be bound up with you in the historic work of the final liberation of China and other exploited countries from the yoke of imperialism. . . . Taking leave of you, my dear comrades, I want to express the hope that the day will come when the USSR will welcome a friend and ally in a mighty free China and that in the great struggles for the liberation of the oppressed peoples of the world both these allies will go forward to victory hand in hand.' Russian experts helped Sun establish the famous military academy of Whampoa. For its head Sun selected one of his promising supporters, a young man named Chiang Kai-shek; his political advisor was another promising young man named Chou En-lai. Chiang was sent to study in Moscow; he had fewer illusions than Sun about the Soviet Union's unselfish concern for the Chinese revolution; the Soviet Union, in turn, had few illusions about Chiang's supposedly unselfish concern for the Chinese revolution.

Nonetheless, both Chiang and Stalin, each for his own reason, worked together throughout the next decades. As Sun's successor and

* It should be noted, also, that the Russian Army was one of the eight foreign armies which occupied and sacked Peking in 1900 during the Boxer Rebellion.

the head of the Nationalist government—the Kuomintang (KMT)—Chiang was given official Russian support. This situation, naturally, produced a curiously mottled relationship between the Chinese Communist Party and its Soviet counterpart. Stalin, wanting a China strong enough to resist Japanese encroachments on his own Far-Eastern sphere of influence, saw in Chiang a stronger ally than the Communist Party (born in secret in 1921) but he failed to measure Mao's stature. Today, China gives Stalin a proud position in the Marxist-Leninist pantheon, yet the record shows that her interests were often subordinated to power struggles between Stalin and his great rival, Trotsky; Russian advice was often misleading and on occasion disastrous.

There were two major lines which the Russians wished the Chinese to follow. First, they were to stay with the Kuomintang and Chiang, working together for the *bourgeois*-democratic revolution (which precedes the Socialist one). Borodin, chief Russian adviser, tendered this advice throughout the 1920s even when Chiang had temporarily arrested Soviet advisers and barred Chinese Communists from the KMT; Mao called him a 'blunderer'. The third congress of the Chinese Party raised the slogan, 'All work to the KMT—it should be the central force of the national revolution and should stand in the leading position', but in Shanghai in 1927, Chiang and the KMT right wing 'betrayed the revolution' when they turned on the workers and Party members supporting their cause and massacred thousands. (Among those who escaped was Chou En-lai.)

Second, the Chinese Communists were to get control of the major cities. Though early efforts ended in bloodshed with thousands of ill-trained, ill-equipped peasant soldiers lying dead before city walls or in the streets, *Pravda* reiterated in 1930: 'We see the inevitability of the extension and strengthening of the Communist Party of China . . . which is now rousing millions of workers and peasants to struggle for national liberation and endeavouring to link up the workers' movements in the industrial centres.' (Chou En-lai has reported that the Party at that time had fewer than four per cent of city workers in its ranks.)

Only nine weeks later, Moscow, in a sudden *volte face*, changed its policy and turned on its 'city line' supporters in the Chinese Party; but the damage had been done and untold lives lost.

During this period Mao Tse-tung seems to have received little, or unfavourable, attention from the Kremlin or its advisers in China. His now famous *Report on the Peasant Movement in Hunan*, 1927, with its cogent arguments for a peasant-oriented revolution, was more than suspect to Russian-influenced Chinese Communists. Nassonov, one of the few dissenting advisers, wrote: 'To the Chinese comrades the peasants are a dull dumb mass. No peasant power can be organised, they say, for it will frighten away the petty *bourgeoisie*.'

The war against Japan brought at least a partial change. It found Mao and the Red Army in Yenan in firm control of large areas of rural China and in firm agreement with Moscow on the need for a strong united front of Communists and Nationalists against the aggressors. Even so, contacts between Yenan and Moscow seemed less frequent than between Moscow and Chungking, Chiang's wartime capital. Because of Chiang's blockade round the 'Red border regions' (to the Communists, these were 'the liberated areas') Russian aid to

China failed to reach the Red guerrillas under Mao and Lin Paio. Ironically, Madam Chiang chided the USA for giving less support than the Soviet Union: 'And Russian help was unconditional throughout.'

The American ambassador reported as early as 1937: 'The USSR has agreed to extend one million Chinese dollars for the purchase of military supplies by the Chiang régime and actual deliveries have exceeded that amount.'

A Communist historian writing before the Sino-Soviet split describes Russian help as that of a good ally, a true friend in need. Stalin hardly behaved like an ally at the Yalta Conference in 1945, for, without consulting Chiang, he signed an agreement with Roosevelt and Churchill whereby, *inter alia*, the 'USSR was to recover the former rights of Russia violated by the treacherous attack of Japan in 1904', including the re-establishment of joint Sino-Soviet control over the railways in Manchuria, the internationalisation of Dairen and the recognition of the separation of Outer Mongolia.[2]

Immediately after the Japanese surrendered, the Russians made haste to dismantle industrial equipment in Manchuria. George Moorad wrote of his journey to Mukden with a group of American journalists. 'Mukden was mile after mile of skeletons and emptiness, shells of buildings, frameworks of factories, in which great holes had been gouged to permit the exit of machinery. . . . It represented 40 per cent of the industry of Manchuria, which in turn was 70 per cent of all industry in China. It produced or handled 4 million tons of steel and iron annually, as well as $3\frac{1}{2}$ million tons of synthetic petroleum. . . . In its giant warehouses, the Japanese said 2 million tons of grain had been stored. Now Mukden looked as if a horde of steel and concrete-eating termites had passed through.'[3]

But relations seemed to remain friendly and in 1949, just before his final victory, Mao made his oft-quoted, lean-to-one-side speech— China was to lean to the Socialist side.

As Stalin's prestige diminished following his death, Mao's increased, and he was even referred to in the USSR as 'the number one Communist'. Kruschev, bent on destroying the Stalin image, at first accepted this. With obvious relish he summarised Stalin's mistakes in China. 'It has been the lack of faith on Stalin's part in our Chinese comrades which led to an unnecessary retarding of their positive programme for the establishment of popular democracy and the elimination of the disastrous régime of Chiang Kai-shek and his *bourgeois*, imperialist collaborators.' In the opinion of Stalin's successor the blame was placed squarely where it belonged.

The Chinese, by this time, were less than grateful for retrospective sympathy from the Russian who had become the chief 'revisionist'.

Looking back on this period of Sino-Soviet relations in September 1963 the editorial department of the *People's Daily* and the *Red Flag* cogently analysed Stalin's role in Soviet and Chinese history during the 1930s and 1940s from the Chinese point of view. The article made clear why, in spite of everything, Stalin's larger-than-life portrait shares the honours at all Chinese national celebrations with Marx, Engels, Lenin and even Mao himself.

'The Communist Party of China has consistently held that Stalin did commit errors . . . and it is necessary to criticise the errors he made. But we have consistently opposed improper criticism . . . Stalin fought tsarism and propagated Marxism during Lenin's lifetime; he took part in the struggle to pave the way for the 1917 Revolution . . . His merits and mistakes are a matter of objective reality . . . His merits outweighed his faults. He was primarily correct and his faults were secondary.' Today, for Maoists, the judgement still stands.[4]

Areas taken by Russia in the nineteenth century. 'The more inert countries in Asia will fall prey to the powerful invaders and will be divided up between them . . . especially . . . the Chinese colossus. Russia, both geographically and historically, has the undisputed right to the lion's share of the expected prey.' (Russian Minister, Sergei Witte)

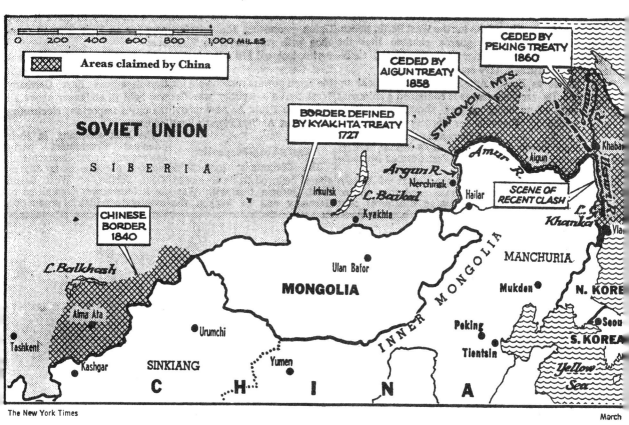

The New York Times

March

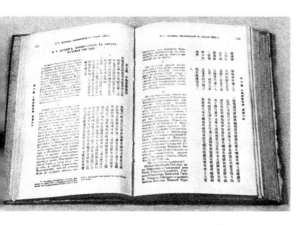

Sino-Russian Treaty of Aigun, 1858. 'While the allied Anglo-French troops were committing aggression against China, tsarist Russian imperialism seized the opportunity to compel the Chiang dynasty . . . to sign the Unequal Treaty of Aigun in 1858. By this treaty it annexed Chinese territory north of the Heilung River, an area of over 600 000 square kilometres, and placed a vast expanse of Chinese territory east of the Wusuli River under the joint control of China and Russia. . . . In 1869 Russian imperialism forced the Chiang dynasty to sign another unequal treaty, the Treaty of Peking, 1860, by which it forcibly incorporated into Russia all the territory east of the Wusuli, about 400 000 square kilometres . . . [they] used coercion to occupy a total of 1 000 000 square kilometres in North-eastern China, an area twice as big as France.' (*Down With The New Tsars*, F.L.P.)

Russian troops. 'Naturally Russia is most convenient for us, because England uses commerce to absorb the profits of China, France uses religion to entice the Chinese people, Germany has no common territorial boundary with us, and the United States does not like to interfere in others' military affairs. . . . If China and Russia form an alliance, English influence will be considerably curbed and Russia would be willing to accommodate us.' (Memorial to the Emperor from Chang Chih-tung, 1895)

A Russian military hospital during the Russo-Japanese War.

Russians sacking a temple during the Boxer Rebellion.

'Port Arthur [now Lüshan] is chiefly a military capital. Its main business centre and its seaport, ... will be the newly-created city of Dalny. ... In the center a monumental exhibition pavilion will adorn the future "Nicholas Square" and from there, radiating like the points of a star, ten broad avenues will originate leading to public buildings such as Orthodox, Catholic or Protestant churches, museums, a theatre, a library and schools. This will be the city's business and industrial section, and it will contain huge buildings housing the warehouses. In the immediate vicinity of the Chinese quarter, a large bazaar with railroad connections will be the focal point for all traffic, as well as the center of exchange between Europeans and Chinese.' (French Military Mission Report)

A *Punch* cartoon: 'Paws Off'. 'The European governments (the Russian government among the very first) have already partitioned China. However, they have not begun partitioning openly, but stealthily, like thieves.' (Lenin)

Sun Yat-sen and Chiang Kai-shek, first commandant of the Whampoa Military Academy, established with Soviet help in 1924.

Sun Yat-sen.

Chiang Kai-shek in Moscow. 'The sole aim of the Russian party is to make the Chinese Communist Party its legitimate heir. They do not believe that our party could cooperate with them in the least. They want to make Manchuria, Mongolia, the Mohammedan Province and Tibet each a part of their Soviet and even as to China proper they are not without a wish to put their fingers in.' (Chiang Kai-Shek, 1924) The Russians said of Chiang 'We consider him to be an individual of outstanding characteristics; the principal one is an inordinate desire for glory. . . . His actual understanding of the problems of revolution is quite another thing. His desire to take advantage of the Revolution makes him veer to and fro between the Right and the Communists.' And Stalin advised: 'None can guarantee that Chiang Kai-shek will always be one of us but we must utilise him and co-operate with him to the very end.' (Comment by Russian adviser in Peking)

The massacre in Shanghai in 1927. 'Stalin is the gravedigger of the Chinese Revolution . . . to enter the KMT meant to bring one's head voluntarily to the slaughter. The bloody lessons of Shanghai passed without leaving a trace. The Communists as before were being transformed into cattle-herders for the party of the *bourgeois* executioners.' (Trotsky)

Following his *coup d'etat* against the revolution on 12 April 1927, Chiang Kai-shek ordered the arrest and deaths of hundreds of workers and progressives in Shanghai and other cities.

所謂蘇維埃政府佈告及其產黨標語

湖南省政府已成瓦礫之場
The wreck of the Hunan Provincial House

路上行人被紅軍槍殺後慘狀
A victim lying on the street

住宅遭毀拆居民流離失所
The demolished houses after the raid

被焚後之湖南省黨部
The Hunan Provincial Kuomintang Office was also being burned down

'The Red Army must be strengthened and organised so that it may be able to take over more and more key cities in the future . . . the Red Army must struggle to capture Changsha and Nanchang and then Hankow. Finally, it must carry on down the Yangtse to Shanghai.' (Commintern Directive)

Headquarters of the Nanchang uprising. The city of Nanchang was seized by Chu Teh during the night of 31 July 1927. The rebels had to abandon Nanchung on 5 August and retreat south.

Chinese regard for Marx, Engels, Lenin and Stalin
has not wavered over the years, for Stalin led the
CPSU and Soviet people in 'safeguarding the first
Socialist state in the world . . . and led the Soviet
army to the victory of the anti-Fascist war'. Here,
young people read in a modern library, under
portraits of the four men. 'We have made mistakes.
We have told the Chinese comrades frankly that
we felt the prospects of revolt in China were nil
and that they should seek a *modus vivendi* with
Chiang Kai-shek, take part in his government and
disband their army. We admit we were wrong.
It turned out that the Chinese comrades were right
and not the Soviets.' (Stalin, 1938)

'It always surprised us in Yenan that we didn't
see any Russians hiding under the bushes. We
felt that they must be there, you see, giving orders
to Mao Tse-tung . . . although we began to decide
in our own minds that this just probably wasn't
so, because Mao obviously was a great Communist
figure in his own right, and he was not about to
take orders from Stalin or anyone else.' (John
Emerson)

II   China and Japan

*apan wants to lead the East in war, in commerce, and in
nufactures, and next century will be a hard one for the
est! Everything that China should have yielded gracefully
 others when asked for will now have to be yielded to
pan's hectoring. Japan will then pose and say to all creat-
—"That's the way to do it, you see, and it's I that did
'.' (Sir Robert Hart, 1905)*

*hairman Mao has pointed out that among the Japanese,
ept for the pro-US capitalists and the militarists, the
ad masses of the people are our friends.'*
eking People's Daily, 1971)

7 China and Japan

Since the US withdrawal from Asia has become apparent and the revived power of Japan a probability, China's fears of Japan, once allayed by the defeat of the former expansionist Japanese Empire, have revived. It is thought possible, if not likely, that the new US 'Guam Doctrine' (which implies that Asian countries opposed to Communism should provide their own defence) also suggests that Japan should fill the role which US power has played since the end of World War II. China regards this possibility as a threat, and one enhanced by the strength and growth of the Japanese economy, which since the end of World War II has carried only a very light burden of armament costs. On the other hand Japan is an important trading partner for China, and trade has grown steadily in spite of the absence of diplomatic relations. Japanese industrialists visit China in large numbers and are freely admitted; Japanese political leaders below the level of Prime Minister have also visited China. It is widely believed that only US persuasion has prevented Japan from entering into diplomatic relations with China and recognising the Peking government. Very many Japanese, including many capitalists and entrepreneurs, deplore the fact that there are no diplomatic relations between the two countries.

As neighbours, bound closely by the facts of geography and reinforced by a common heritage of civilisation which has had many links throughout the ages, China and Japan are destined to be either friends or foes. Indifference, or aloofness, are not in the long run possible for either country. The history of the past confirms this fact. When Japan first borrowed from China the literary culture of the Tang period (from the seventh to tenth centuries AD) and with it the Buddhist religion, cultural ties were very close, and political enmity negligible. For the greater part of the succeeding centuries this was the normal relationship. The Mongol conquerors of China (not the Chinese) attempted to invade Japan at the end of the fourteenth century, but were twice successfully repulsed; but at much the same period there was a further, strong Chinese influence upon the culture of Japan, brought by traders and by scholars and monks who fled abroad from the Mongol conquest. This created new ties between the two countries, and during the subsequent Chinese Ming period Chinese philosophers were read and studied in Japan as much as in China itself. The Japanese invasion of Korea in the late sixteenth century brought about a war between the two countries, with indecisive results, except that the Japanese withdrew from the peninsula kingdom. From that time until the late nineteenth century, relations between China and Japan were peaceful, if somewhat restricted since Japan was closed to all but a very small trickle of trade. On the other hand, cultural relations continued.

It is therefore rather deceptive to speak of China and Japan as 'traditional enemies'. The occasions before modern times on which there was a clash of arms between them were very rare and separated by centuries. No such peaceful record distinguishes the history of European neighbour nations. In response to foreign pressure Japan adopted modern nationalism and material civilisation with vigour and determination at the end of the nineteenth century, proving herself an apt pupil of the colonial and imperial European powers. Aggression against the failing Manchu Empire provided the scope and target for such ambitions. In 1895, as a consequence of the war she fought in Korea against China, Japan acquired Taiwan and terminated Chinese suzerainty over Korea, substituting her own.

If France and Russia had not intervened and forced her to relinquish the Manchurian port cities of Lushan and Talienwan (Port Arthur and Dairen) in favour of Russia, she would have added these spoils to her territory.

In 1900, following the Boxer Rebellion, Japan secured equal status in China with the other Treaty Powers. In 1904–5 she defeated Russia in a war fought on Chinese territory in Manchuria, and reaped her reward by taking over the Russian concessions in the ports, and wide rights to build and police new railways. In 1915, although China was able to reject the more oppressive of the Twenty-one Demands made upon her by Japan, she had to accept many which greatly increased Japan's hold on the economy in Manchuria and also on the political and military balance there. These trends were consummated by the outright seizure of the whole of Manchuria in 1931, and followed by steady encroachment into North China and Inner Mongolia. The end of this series of aggressions was the general invasion of China in 1937, and the occupation of nearly one-third of the country, a situation which provoked the guerrilla war conducted by the Communist Party, and did not end until the Japanese surrender to the Allies in 1945.

Thus, the peaceful relations of an earlier epoch gave way to continuous hostility and frequent open warfare for fifty years. In spite of these enmities, relations between the two countries were often close in other fields. Japan, the first to modernise, became the transmitter of much of the modern, originally Western, technology and science. Chinese terms for many modern institutions, activities and artifacts are taken from Japanese usage, for both countries shared the Chinese ideographic script and mutual borrowing was natural and simple. Many hundreds or even thousands of Chinese students completed their education in Japan, which was nearer and cheaper than Europe or the USA. Throughout the period of active political hostility and even that of military conflict, the cultural impact of modern Japan upon China was strong. Yet it was limited; China took modern terminology for science and technology, and Chinese students found relatively cheap higher education, but the students working in conservative and imperial Japan were themselves dedicated revolutionary republicans in respect of their own country. The science and the technology were acceptable, but Japan's political system and national outlook were totally rejected. No Chinese reformer sought a Japanese model for a new political programme; Japanese chauvinistic nationalism had few if any Chinese admirers or imitators. This selective approach is also manifest in the Chinese response to Western influences.

In the late nineteenth century, and even more in the early decades of the twentieth, China's failure to model herself on Japan was a favourite subject of Western criticism, which became somewhat muted when Japan developed into the major threat to the position of the Western powers themselves; but in essence it revealed the strength and coherence of the Chinese civilisation and sense of national identity. China could not easily borrow; she had to adapt to make innovations acceptable and workable. It is this national characteristic, together with contingent circumstances such as the great size of China and rule at the relevant period by an alien and weakening dynasty, which is the real cause of the time-lag in the modernisation of China and Japan. It is a difference which is rapidly ceasing to be significant; in fifty years time it will only be remembered by historians specialising in this period.

Memories of Japanese exploitation and militarism are kept alive by oft-repeated stories of Chinese valour during the Japanese occupation and the Anti-Japanese War. Several of the most popular stage performances, operas, ballets and plays deal with this period; children's tales and newspaper comic strips recount anti-Japanese deeds during the long struggle to set China free. It would seem that while national expression of these sentiments is not great, it has created barriers to closer understanding and co-operation. This is evident in China's statements since 1950, especially over the last two or three years. At the same time, Peking has shown a determination to make a start. The Chinese hope for rapprochement is based primarily on the Maoist distinction between government and people: the former may be antagonistic but the people, the masses, share a common desire for peace and co-operation and an end to militarism.

Two important sections of the Japanese people, both opposing more military developments which might lead to further disastrous military adventures, have long sought rapprochement with China. These are the young students and workers, and the merchants. Many young people see Marxism-Leninism and Mao Tsetung's Thought as a solution to their problems just as the Chinese youth of the last century sought in Japan the way to end their outmoded dynastic system. But the Maoists are not a large or influential group; the main link between the two Far Eastern powers is trade. The two countries are complementary economies in many ways. Japan, poor in natural resources, seeks minerals, agricultural produce and a market for some of her consumer goods; China seeks a similar market, and wants to buy as much heavy industrial machinery as Japan can sell her and she can afford to buy. Japanese traders flock to the twice-yearly Canton Fairs in ever increasing numbers. In 1970 Japan's exports to China were worth $US 569 million and imports from China $US 254 million.

Politicians, not only of the far left, who are now urging all possible trade agreements, still face strong opposition from the old guard who fought long and hard for a continuation of the military pacts between the US, Taiwan and Japan.

Robert Guillain made the position clear in March 1971: 'The return from Peking of the Japanese mission sent to renew the Sino-Japanese Trade Agreement has considerably sharpened the debate in Tokyo on Japan's policy towards China. The delegation was composed of pro-Peking politicians, the most prominent being Aichiro Fujiyama, a former foreign minister, who sits in the Diet. The renewed agreement seems even more promising than was initially expected, but it has been given a very chilly reception in some quarters coming out strongly in favour of closer links with China. Mr Fujiyama . . . argues that Tokyo must immediately recognise the People's Republic as the only legitimate Chinese government. The 1952 Treaty between Taiwan and Japan . . . must be denounced.'[1]

But the Chinese, who see the militaristic tradition as still tenacious, and the US as still abetting its followers, felt their fears strongly reinforced by the US return of the island of Okinawa to Japan in 1972—an Okinawa that still has atomic weapons and military bases in American control.

In 1970 Alexis B. Johnson, Under-Secretary to the US State

Department, revealed that the USA regarded Japan as the core of the 'security network' for the whole of South-east Asia. Many people in all countries of the area saw this as a very dangerous concept. 'It seems clear to me,' said Johnson, 'that the relationship between the United States and Japan, and Japan's position in and relationship to the other countries of Asia, is going to continue to be an increasingly crucial factor in the development in that vast area which is of such importance to the United States. The Japanese recognise that the security of Japan cannot be separated from that of Korea, Taiwan and our obligations elsewhere in the area, and thus, in looking at the question of our bases and facilities in Japan, they will look at it in terms of the security of the whole area rather than in the security just of Japan itself.' China, deeply concerned, bitterly criticised the statement.

For years the Chinese showed concern at Japanese rearmament with US collaboration and in September 1971 the Communist *Ta Kung Pao* pointed out from Hong Kong: 'Today the total number of Japan's "Self-defence Forces" is more than at any time since the 18 September "Incident" of 1931. Her fire power is ten times as much as that before World War II. Sato and company have declared openly that "Korea is essential to Japan's security" and that China's Taiwan "province" is also a most important factor for the security of Japan. They flagrantly include China's Tiaoyu and other islands in "the scope of Japanese defence" declaring that Japan will use force to "defend" these islands.'

Robert Guillain stated the problem squarely in *Le Monde* in August 1971: 'One senses very strongly in Peking that the problem of the growing strength of the new Japan now becomes increasingly sharp. May not the pressure, which has decreased in the south, become stronger in the north? Will not Japan see in the American retreat an opportunity for a thrust in the Pacific? . . . In Tokyo these fears may seem absurd or artificial. In Peking one is struck by their obvious sincerity. When China denounces, as she has done since 1970 . . . "the re-birth of Japanese militarism" she is motivated by an authentic fear based on an analysis of the facts which one cannot lightly reject. . .

'Mr Chou En-lai points out for each of his foreign visitors these days the existence of a Japanese danger. It is the fatal consequence, he explains, of the blind rush of big Japanese capital towards becoming an economic super-power. In a highly significant way he shows the military danger closely allied with the disordered and excessive rise of Japanese economic strength.

'Japan has no need to be so strong and to climb so high, is what he is saying in substance. Her growth is excessive and unbalanced.

'Finally, from Peking one can see more clearly than ever before a Japan faced with a major choice, either to inherit and continue the anti-China policy of containment and expect a long period of confrontation, or to "throw on the scrap-heap" the former policy, and to replace this by a new policy, a Japanese policy, which would seek in her own way a *détente* and perhaps collaboration.'

It is therefore clear that one of the more important of the complex of reasons for the American President's visit to China was China's desire that the USA lessen her support for the Japanese militants, the anti-China lobby and, by implication, the Japanese-Taiwan alliance.

China's very real concern about this alliance was made clear in a strong statement in *New China News* in May 1972. 'The May issue of the Japanese journal *Military Research* carried an article by a commentator, Chu Saito . . . which once again lays bare the wild ambitions of the Japanese militarist forces. Chu Saito asserted: "Taiwan has a stranglehold on the maritime trade route which maintains Japan's life" and "the loss of Taiwan will directly endanger the fate of Japan and the Republic of Korea." Anyone knows well that whenever Japanese militarism wanted to invade a country it always claimed that the territory of that country was "its lifeline". Is not Chu Saito's present outcry . . . the logic of fascist pirates, exactly the same as that of the notorious "Tanaka's memorial to the throne"?'

President Nixon's all-important visit took the Japanese by surprise —and not pleasantly so. It seemed that a major victory (for the Chinese) came soon after when Prime Minister Sato of Japan described Taiwan as 'indisputably part of the People's Republic of China'. But such was the consternation caused that he and his supporters sought later to qualify or contradict the statement, and thoroughly confused the issue.

China, too, was far from accepting Mr Sato's statement at its face value. In March 1972, China's press launched a strong attack on Prime Minister Sato, accusing him of plotting aggressive moves on China's territory of Taiwan, and the Ministry of Foreign Affairs made it abundantly clear that there could be no dealings with the Japanese government while Mr Sato was Prime Minister.

'In his 19 October 1971 speech Prime Minister Sato, to facilitate his US masters' continued occupation of Okinawa, aimed at railroading through the Okinawa Reversion Agreement. . . . This agreement is simply a fraud with no explicit agreement for the removal of US nuclear weapons or troops from Okinawa.' (*Peking Review*) Here, a rally and demonstration against turning Japan into a US military base is being held in Sasebo.

Japanese demonstrators holding an anti-US demonstration in 1971. 'As the Chinese see it there are two Japans . . . the Japan of Sato and that of the Japanese people. On the one hand Sato and the pro-US monopolies talk about Korea and Taiwan being their vital interests. . . . On the other hand there are the Japanese people who do not want wars of conquest but want peace and friendship with the Chinese people. They crave and are fighting for a Japan which is independent and neutral.' (*Ta Kung Pao*)

Chinese trade personnel talking business with Japanese merchants.

Sato's dilemma. 'Japan is not in a position to speak on Taiwan's status in connection with the San Francisco Peace Treaty, but we can understand the PRC's claim that Taiwan is part of it. Therefore the government will make positive efforts to normalise relations with China based on this understanding.'

Japanese troops. The question now confronting Japan is whether to take the road of war or take the road of peace. Taking the road of economic expansion will inevitably lead to military expansion and give rise to war. The other road is to establish an independent, neutral, peaceful and democratic Japan; such a Japan will be welcome.' (Chou En-lai, 1971)

Shachiapang, a Peking opera of the Japanese war period, is set in the early days of the war of resistance against Japan. Puppet troops arrive to look for eighteen wounded soldiers left behind by the New Fourth Army to recover in the village of Shachiapang. There is a majestic overture in praise of Chairman Mao and the Communist Party leading the Chinese people to fight the Japanese and save the nation. The marching song of the Red Army is used as the theme melody:

Red flags fly; the bugles sound,
Hills and rivers echo.
Drive out the Japanese invaders,
Wipe out the traitors.

Red Signal Lantern, another Peking opera, tells the story of a railway signalman, his mother and daughter, all of whom work with the guerrillas against the Japanese, and are eventually captured. Both mother and son are tortured and killed. A Deputy Company Leader of a naval unit said about it: 'When we listened to the vigorous strains of the Red Lantern Peking Opera singing, we were deeply moved. It took us back to the days of the war of resistance against the Japanese, bringing to our minds the brutal Japanese imperialists and their atrocities.'

9 China and Japan: Confrontation

It was not until the very end of the nineteenth century that an increasingly powerful Japan cast covetous eyes upon her neighbour. In 1894 her modern army and navy moved against both Korea and China.

The long, sad story of these Sino-Japanese relations can best start with a much-celebrated incident in the first major Japanese attack in September 1894, the great naval battle fought and lost on the Yellow Sea known as the Battle of Tatungjou. China admitted defeat and signed the humiliating Treaty of Shimonoseki, by which she paid heavy indemnities and ceded large tracts of territory, the most important being the island of Taiwan. The Taiwanese refused to accept their fate and fought land and sea battles for several months before they surrendered to the Japanese. Their struggle is often proudly recorded by modern historians.

An interesting parallel to Chinese accounts of these various battles is provided by contributors to the *Illustrated London News* in 1894. They make painfully clear the gross inadequacies of the Chinese armies and their inferiority to the Japanese forces: 'There are three main Chinese armies—1. The Eight Banners are all badly armed, 2. The Green Flags or National Army is really a militia of which only one third serves at a time; it is badly organised, 3. The Black Flags of Li Hung-chang is better paid and has modern equipment. The Japanese march well and quickly and can exist on a few spoonfuls of rice a day. The enthusiasm in the Japanese forces and the spectacle of an Eastern nation fighting and manoeuvring with a verve and intelligence worthy of a first-class European war has sent a thrill of admiring wonder through the military world.'

From this time onwards until 1945 China was never to be without Japanese military on her soil; her obvious weakness during the second half of the nineteenth century encouraged the expansionist ambitions of Japan, who, after the Treaty of Shimonoseki, kept coming back for more.

Yet China should have been prepared. In 1874 Wen Hsiang, an important court official and colleague of Prince Kung, prophesied only too accurately what lay ahead. 'Japan, a small country in the eastern ocean, has only lately adopted Western military methods and bought two ironclads; on the basis of these, she has dared to stir up trouble . . . If we continue to drift along passively and do not anxiously try to seek improvement to catch up, trouble in the future will be even more difficult to meet. For this reason, things like ironclads, naval fortresses, etc. must be begun at once. But substantial funds are not available, and besides, purchasing orders take time to fill.' The even more influential Li Hung-chang realised that China and Japan were natural allies, sharing a common culture, a common threat. 'How could we be enemies? Together our Asiatic yellow race will not be encroached upon by the white race of Europe'. But the hope was vain; Japan did not seek friendship and her territorial ambitions grew.

At the turn of the century Sir Robert Hart, English head of the Chinese Customs, prophesied 'a hard century for the West . . . because of Japan's hectoring'. But all warnings went unheeded and Japan's successes at the end of the nineteenth century whetted her appetite for more.

It was inevitable that Japan, casting covetous eyes on the vast reaches of Manchuria, should come into conflict with the equally covetous Russia. Japan was victorious both on land and sea; the land war was fought on Chinese soil and the spoils handed over by the defeated Tsar to the victorious Emperor consisted of Chinese territories and concessions. But, by a truly Maoist contradiction, 'a bad thing became a good thing', for China at last realised what she must do.

An Eastern power had, for the first time in history, defeated a Western one; China, also, had hopes of one day following suit. To do this she must copy Japan's copying of the West. This would be a slow process though, and in the meantime Russia had recognised Japan's paramount interest in Korea (which was to be her spring-board for future anti-China expeditions) and she had transferred to Japan her lease on the Liaotung Peninsula and the railway to Chungchun. For the time, at least, Japan agreed that Manchuria should return to Chinese administration.

Thousands of ardent young Chinese patriots saw Japan's strength, marvelled at her crucial victory over the tsarist forces and hoped to find in Japan a solution for their own country's problems. They flocked to schools and universities in Tokyo and the provincial cities. To their hosts they had an ambivalent attitude; admiring in some ways, they were apprehensive in others and always fiercely independent. Wu Yu-chang, later a member of the Central Committee of the CCP, writes of his Japanese experience: 'When we arrived in Japan there were not many Chinese students there, the total number being only about a thousand. The number of Szechuan students was much smaller. We all felt it necessary to ask the people of our home province to send more students to study overseas... We sent a petition to the provincial authorities asking them to send one or two government-supported students from each county to study in the schools of Japan. This document played a great role in helping the Szechuan people to realise the importance of sending students to study in Japan. By 1905 the number exceeded 10 000 ...

'I remember that on New Year's Day, 1904, when the flags of various countries were hung up in the school, the Chinese flag was conspicuous by its absence. The Chinese students were very indignant and I led them in a determined protest. We told the school authorities that unless they hung up the Chinese flag and apologised we would not attend class and would go on a hunger-strike... Under the impact of the Chinese students' united action the school authorities finally gave in. It had always been the policy of the Japanese imperialists to wheedle and win over the Chinese students by hook or by crook. There were some Chinese students in Japan who were willing to sacrifice principle for profit and who allowed themselves to come under the influence of the Japanese. Some of them later betrayed their country... My hatred of Japanese imperialism increased in direct proportion to its intensification of aggression against China. The struggle against Japanese imperialism and for the existence of the Chinese nation thereafter occupied a prominent place in my life.'

Sun Yat-sen himself lived for a time in Japan, had friends there, and learned much. But he harboured no illusions, which was not surprising when threatening statements such as this ominous one from the Black Dragon Society appeared in 1915 when Sun himself was in Japan. 'When the European war is terminated and peace restored we are not so much concerned with the question whether it be Germany or the Allies which emerge victorious but whether, in anticipation of the future expansion of European influence in the continents of Europe and Asia, the Imperial Japanese government should or should not hesitate to use force [to check the movement]. Now is the most opportune time for Japan to quickly solve the China question. Such an opportunity will not occur again for hundreds of years.'

In January 1915 Japan presented the notorious Twenty-one Demands to Yuan Shih-kai; she sought large territoria/ and industrial concessions as well as a Japanese share in the policing of certain important areas of China. The Twenty-one Demands amounted virtually to one demand—that China become a Japanese protectorate. Many of the demands were acceded to by a Yuan Shih-kai frightened of Japanese aggression.

Japan supported the Allies in World War I and was generously rewarded by them—at the expense of another Ally, China, who had sent thousands to serve in labour corps on the Western Front.

The Treaty of Versailles contained the infamous Clause 156 which transferred to Japan all of defeated Germany's assets and concessions in China. This precipitated the May Fourth Movement which is discussed in Chapter 16. But worse was to come. In 1927 Gichi Tanaka secretly advised his Emperor in the Tanaka Memorial (admittedly of doubtful authenticity): 'If we want to conquer China, we must conquer Manchuria and Mongolia first. If we want to conquer the world, we must conquer China first . . . If we get the right in our hands to control Manchuria and Mongolia, we can use them as a base and conquer China by means of trade. Moreover, we can use Manchuria and Mongolia as headquarters to wrest the rich resources of the entire country with which to conquer India, the South Sea Islands, Central Asia, Asia Minor and Europe. If the Japanese nation attempts to dominate Asia, the first important link lies in getting the right to control Manchuria and Mongolia.'

In an article headed 'No Repetition of the 18 September Incident' a modern Chinese historian taking up the story, describes how Japan concocted an 'incident' on the Manchurian railway to give her an excuse to attack China. He gives examples of Japan's continued encroachments over the next eighteen years: 'In 1932, the Japanese fascists created the Pingtingshan massacre in Fushun . . . Over 3 000 innocent people were bayoneted by the Japanese troops and their homes burned to ashes. All over the north-east they made "ten thousand people pits", filled with the bones of the Chinese people . . . The Japanese also pillaged China of its farm products. . . . On 7 July 1937 the Japanese attacked Lukouchiao, the Marco Polo Bridge, south-west of Peking, unleashing a full scale war to put all of China under its control.' The first Chinese victory over the Japanese was the Battle of Pinghsingkuan Pass in the September of that year.

There were few Nationalist successes against the Japanese during these years. Chiang, 'anti-Red before anti-Jap', fought some engagements, but kept his forces out of major battles with the enemy the better to deal with the hated Communists.

Japan's presence was seen and felt everywhere. The Japanese took over more and more Chinese industry and tried to take over educational and cultural institutions. Many of these were destroyed and thousands of students moved far inland to set up primitive schools and colleges.

Citizens suffered countless iniquities in raids on houses and searches of individuals in shops and streets, in addition to war damage. Shanghai and other Chinese cities were among the first in history to suffer massive aerial bombardment.

Chiang's concept of priorities outraged one of his own generals, the famous Young Marshall, Chang Hsuen-liang, son of Manchurian war-lord Chang Tso-lin. (It was, after all, his country that the enemy occupied.) In November 1936 he appealed to Chiang Kai-shek for an immediate order to all Kuomintang troops to fulfil their sacred mission of fighting the Japanese. Chiang rejected the appeal so the Young Marshall and a fellow general kidnapped him from his hotel near the ancient city of Sian and threatened to kill him outright unless he accepted the Reds' offer of a united front against Japan. Chou En-lai flew from Yenan to Sian where he needed all his diplomatic genius to deal with the situation. Though Chiang agreed to co-operate, his support for the Red Armies was to be reluctant and treacherous. His hatred of them never waned. He did not declare war on Japan until Pearl Harbour brought the US into the war, over four years after China's Anti-Japanese War had opened, in order to avoid application of the US neutrality law which forbade the sale of armaments to combatants openly declared as such.

The English war-correspondent Stuart Gelder described his experience on the Japanese front: 'What was the position in China in the winter of 1943? The Japanese possessed all the ports and major cities. They controlled the entire coastline. The Burma road was closed. They had driven far inland. American military estimates put their total military strength in China at half a million men. These were well trained, clothed and fed and adequately equipped . . . The Chinese Kuomintang Government forces under Chiang Kai-shek were officially reported to number between two million and three million men. Of these, half a million were employed in blockading the Communists in the north and preventing any intercourse between them and the rest of free China. They were never in action against the Japanese . . . Every weapon and bullet that did not go to the Fourteenth Air Force or "Y" Force was delivered to the Kuomintang Government. Not one was ever sent to the Communists from the time America entered the war to the defeat of Japan. [He then goes on to recount Japan's increasingly desperate efforts to wipe out the Chinese guerrilla forces which, as he said, were regarded as a greater threat than the Nationalist armies.] The Prisoner's Cage Tactic was a stratagem designed to bottle up the Chinese in a small area so that the Japanese could move in at will in criss-crossing columns and wipe out all troops caught in their box . . . the Japanese built connecting ditches along railways and roads, twenty feet wide and to the depth of moats. Then across roads and fields about the area they wanted to attack they erected earth walls. So long and numerous were these walls that Po estimated they would go around the earth one and a half times if put end to end. If this seems exaggerated, I can only offer the testimony of my own eyes . . . Yet the Japanese did not succeed in annihilating the forces opposing them. So, in the winter of 1941 and the spring of 1942, they began to burn and kill everything and everyone in their path.' Thousands died, thousands more were homeless refugees, many doomed to die of cold, starvation or exhaustion. Still Chiang would not fight against the foreign enemy.

During the late 1930s China had fought the Japanese alone but with the attack on Pearl Harbour she found herself side by side with the Western Allies and every kind of military material flowed to help Chiang's forces against the invaders. Senior American advisers arrived in Chungking, the best-known being General Joseph Stilwell. He and the rest found Chiang still 'anti-Red before anti-Jap', in spite of the appalling atrocities of the Japanese 'kill, loot all, burn all' policy.

General Stilwell, among others, deplored Chiang's half-heartedness and the corruption of his administration. He suspected Chiang and some of his ministers of secret negotiations with the Japanese, as he recorded periodically in his diaries and confidential reports: 'July 10 Russki rumor: Yuan Liang and party here with peace terms. Also a Jap, Kuoda: Chinese to go back to Nanking [the pre-war capital of China]. Wang Ching-wei to set up in north China. Japs keep Canton, Hangchow, Shanghai. Possibilities. Sympathy here for the Nazis. Same type of government, same outlook, same gangsterism. The howl of "Beat Japan First" has two possible explanations—one, that if it is done, that lets China coast in without effort on her part: and two, that diversions of American effort to the Pacific would relieve Germany of worry about a second front, and perhaps enable her to get a decision from Russia, Chiang Kai-shek would prefer to see Germany win than to end up with a powerful Russia at his door, backing up the Eighteenth Army Group [the Chinese Communist Army]. Which, by the way, has spread pretty well all over North China.'[1]

Stilwell's suspicions were not unjustified, according to R. J. Butow in his book, *Japan's Decision to Surrender*: 'In September 1943 Japanese Ambassador Tani reported than Chiang told him he wished to abandon his wartime policy of co-operation with the Communists so that he could destroy the Party and bring its following under his control. To do this he would have to stop fighting the Japanese and so wanted them to withdraw. If Japan did this he might consider severing relations with the US and Great Britain. Tojo told puppet Wang Ching-wei he had no objections to continuing peace talks but Chiang Kai-shek had to break with the UK and US.'

There is ample documentation, both Chinese and foreign, of collaboration not only by Chiang's military and political officers, but also by some of the comprador class, the larger landlords, and at lower levels among the rich peasants and minor officials. Such traitors feature frequently in modern popular stories, including those written for children.

While Stilwell and the Young Marshall did what they could with the Nationalist leaders and armies, the Communists were waging guerrilla warfare over a vast area of northern China, mostly behind enemy lines. Regular guerrilla troops were helped by great numbers of men, women and even children, fighting, in Mao's famous phrase, a 'people's war'. Fed, clothed and guided by country people, the Red Army men were joined everywhere they went by local militia. To rally all these people behind them the Communists issued a ten point anti-Japanese programme, not only for carrying out guerrilla warfare and establishing anti-Japanese bases, but also for an immediate land reform programme and reduction of crippling interest rates.

Guerrilla operations were based on Mao's military writing on guerrilla warfare and his important treatise *On Protracted War*. In this he foretold a long haul to final victory, defining the three stages of strategic defence, strategic stalemate and strategic counter-offensive.

Three harassing techniques developed successfully by the guerrillas, 'sparrow warfare', tunnel warfare and railway sabotage, kept tens of thousands of Japanese troops continually on the alert. The exploits of the guerrillas are today's most popular reading in the People's Republic—the subject of children's 'comics', the theme of plays, films and musicals, of poems and paintings.

The women, too, played their part in the war effort, forming self-defence corps and performing other duties. 'Men and women converged on Yenan like numerous mountain streams. They had come from far-away villages in the surrounding hills carrying red flags and waving red-tasselled spears. As they marched they raised their arms and shouted, "Down with Japanese imperialism". Some sang militant songs denouncing the Japanese invaders.

'Our company of 100 strong was led by a young girl about nineteen years old. The women looked trim and soldierly with their red tasselled spears and swinging stride. At the review they acquitted themselves well, marching in various formations and even giving a demonstration of target drill and bayonet practice. Their other activities included sentry duty, patrolling, delivering messages, acting as guides and escorting captured spies, and such things.'[2]

An account by Jack Belden, in *China Shakes the World*, illustrates the kind of occurrence that, multiplied hundreds of times over, prepared the way for another civil war; for the Red Armies, after years of fierce endeavour, were in no mood to hand over to the treacherous Chiang. It also explains the rising tide of anti-KMT feeling amongst the civilian population and the disintegration of morale amongst the military: 'Soon after Fan's group took the final step by going over, lock, stock and barrel to the Japanese. This was by no means an isolated incident. In the late years of the Anti-Japanese War the surrender of whole KMT units intact with their arms was arranged over and over again by high ranking Nationalist officers. In the Taihung Mountains General Pang Ping-hsun went over with all his troops in May 1943, and was appointed chief of the Honan-Shantung Communist Extermination Army. They took up garrison duty at strategic points where they would be in a position to take over control of all the occupied areas [i.e. Red areas] once the Japanese were brought to their knees by forces outside China. Chiang was turning his attention to post-war control of China.'

In 1944–5 the Red Armies, working, though uneasily at that time, with the Nationalist forces, moved over to positional warfare. For China and the Allies the end of the war came when the atomic bomb fell on Hiroshima, but for China there was no peace. The uneasy KMT-CCP alliance fell apart and civil war rent the country for a further four long years.

98

...eet of Japanese ships flying the American flag ...ned towards the Chinese coast, lowered the ...as they heard China's Peiyang Naval Squadron, ...up Japanese flags and opened devastating gun-... A Chinese ship, the *Chihyuan*, was damaged. ...aptain shouted to his men. "It is glorious to ...ighting on the sea" and ordered the ship to ...n full speed ahead and ram the enemy ships. ...*Chihyuan* was struck by a torpedo and all aboard ... killed.' (*Concise History of China*, F.L.P.)

...he September 17 battle the cruiser *Chih Yuen*, ...mour-plated vessel with decks of steel 4 inches ..., built on the Tyne, shot out of line without ...s and made for a Japanese ship to ram her; ...n she did and the Japanese ship sank. Shortly ...wards the *Chih Yuen* herself sank.' (*Illustrated* ...*n News*, 1894)

'In January 1895 the Japanese blockaded Weiha
in Shantung when the entire Peiyang Squac
under pressure from British "advisers" surrend
to the enemy. In March Japan laid down b
conditions as the price of peace and Li Hung-ca
signed the Treaty of Shimonoseki as drawn u
the Japanese.' (*Concise History of China*, F.L.P.)

'Japanese troops landed at Chemulpo in Kore
9 September; 2 000 men in transports from
cruiser *Tayeama Kan* were carried in Korean j
The cruiser has very good equipment of a we
pattern. The men are well shod and each ca
a spare pair of boots and has a knapsac
bullock hide. 10 000 more are to come inclu
the Imperial Guard with the Crown Princ
major of cavalry.' (*Illustrated London News*, 1

Himeji Castle. Chinese architectural forms were adapted by the Japanese. 'In Asia, our two countries, Japan and China, are the closest neighbours and moreover we have the same language. How could we be enemies?' (Li Hung-chang, to the Japanese Premier, 1895)

Japanese troops. 'Japan wants to lead the East in war, in commerce, and in manufactures, and next century will be a hard one for the West! Everything that China should have yielded gracefully to others, when asked for, will now have to be yielded to Japan's hectoring.' (Sir Robert Hart, 1905)

Japan and Korea.

The Marco Polo Bridge Incident. Marco Polo Bridge today. It was from here that Japan started its all-out war of aggression against China on 7 July 1937.

'On 25 September 1937 the 115th Division of the Eighth Route Army under the command of Comrade Lin Piao annihilated 3 000 troops of Japan's crack Itagaki Division at Pinghsingkuan Pass. It was the first major victory of the war. It smashed the Japanese imperialists' wild scheme that "China will be subjugated in three months".' (*Ta Kung Pao*)

The Manchurian Incident. 'Around 10 o'clock on the night of 18 September 1931, the Japanese Kwangtung Army blew up their own South Manchurian Railway in the north-western suburbs of Shenyang and blamed it on Chinese soldiers. On this pretext they launched a surprise attack on Peitaying, thus unleashing their war of aggression.'

抗日與勤共

Anti-Japanese & Anti-Red Campaigns

Gen. Feng Chan-hai's machine gun corps.

Part of the mountain guns captured by Gen. Feng's soldiers from the Japanese.

Militia organized after the Red-occupied district was restored.

Silver dollars issued by the Reds.

The Inspecting Commission giving a speech to the Peace Preservation Corps on ... after the Red-occupied district was restored.

Captured material published by the Nationalists in their Anti-Jap, Anti-Red campaign.

The Nationalist South-west University: a 'classroom'!

Chinese citizens being searched by Japanese soldiers.

Chou En-lai (in white helmet) is greeted at the Yenan airport on his return from the discussion following the Sian Incident.

Pit coolies in Japanese mines. 'I saw children who emerged from the dark shafts almost completely naked, their thin bodies showing through their skins . . . carrying on an average 35 pound loads. The boys looked not older than nine or ten although there were some fourteen and fifteen year olds among them. Their usual pay was ten—twenty cents a day.' (*Chinese Family and Society*, by Olga Lang)

Street fighting in Manchuria: 'The smell of burnt timbers mingles with the acrid smell of roasting human flesh. . . . Vicious fires eat into what yet remains undamaged. . . . Under the spilt tile and brick, beneath the massed timbers, lie hundreds of buried men, women and small girls and boys. . . . I begin to understand the meaning of the Japanese communiqués. "Our naval planes", said Admiral Shimada, "succeeded in accomplishing their purpose with good effect on nearby villages of the enemy." ' (*China Weekly Review* 1932)

Japanese officers.

誰使他們，喪失了爹和娘？誰使他們，這輩了可愛的家鄉，誰使他們，誰踢地踏上無盡的是路？誰使他們流浪？誰存着狼毒的心腸？

A Nationalist boy soldier. The Japanese slogan was: 'Kill all, Burn all, Loot all'. 'As they moved into an area on their mopping-up campaigns, they killed all young men, destroyed or stole all cattle and broke or made off with all farmers' tools and grain. Their object was to create a no-man's land in which nothing could live. At the same time they reinforced their economic blockade, halted all salt and cloth from entering the guerrilla regions and tried to starve the population out of resistance.' (*China Shakes the World*, by J. Belden)

A small refugee.

Victory in sight. Shanhaikuan, an important pass to North-east China, was liberated by the Eighth Route Army in August 1945.

Guerrillas in the Shansi-Chahar-Hopei area destroyed railway lines in order to cut off supplies to the Japanese troops.

Sparrow warfare. In this, guerrillas 'scattered like sparrows over wide areas, appearing and disappearing unexpectedly in order to surprise the enemy forces'. Here, guerrilla fighters study politics during an interval between battles in the Anti-Japanese War. (*China Pictorial*)

'A New Kind of Warfare'
Tunnel warfare, war underground,
Houses and villages linked together,
Thousands of fighters in ambush
Striking terror in the enemy's heart.
Everyone a soldier, everyone fighting,
We'll destroy the invaders to the last man.

Women in central Hopei Province dig tunnels. 'In 1942 the Japanese aggressors . . . surrounded the village of Kaoping in Hopei Province with forts. The village people dug almost a hundred tunnels forming a network which spread to all corners of the village and beyond; fortifications were built at street intersections and on roofs. All the people—men, women and children—became fighters. On 23 March 1945, 3 000 Japanese and puppet troops [Chinese collaborating with Japanese] moved towards the village under cover of a moon-less night planning to destroy the tunnels and occupy the village. They were discovered by the militia sentinels, and the villagers, 2 000 in all, vanished into the tunnels. The Japanese found notices like "Beware of Mines" and "Safety Limit" all around the village. The bewildered enemy dared not move a step and started shelling at random. At midday by pretending to retreat the militia lured the enemy to the south of the village where they stepped on a mine field. The militia then removed the camouflage from the front of the tunnel outlets and the aggressors were forced to flee for their lives. (*China Pictorial*)

Destroying the ditches built by the enemy. 'Going across the plain, I saw so many pillboxes, ditches and walls that it is almost inconceivable that the Chinese could have existed in the midst of them. Once the walls were erected, the Japanese would build roads between railway lines and forts all along the roads. Then they would gradually close in on all areas, cutting up the prison like bean curd so that in the end there was no territory anywhere larger than ten miles in which Chinese troops could operate.' (*China Shakes the World*, by J. Belden)

The women's contribution is especially celebra
Here, women make land mines.

Sending grain to the army
The mule carts are lined up.
Load the grain and fodder!
Let's go without delay
The Fighting Eighth is waiting. (Women's s

Members of children's corps on lookout duty. 'Men and Women converged on Yenan like numerous mountain streams. They had come from far-away villages in the surrounding hills carrying red flags and waving red-tasselled spears. The women looked trim and soldierly . . . At the review they acquitted themselves well, marching in various formations and even giving a demonstration of target drill and bayonet practice. Their other activities included sentry duty, patrolling, delivering messages, acting as guides and escorting captured spies, and such things.' (*Women of China*, F.L.P.)

Members of the Chinese Communist forces laying mines during the war against the Japanese in the early 1940s.

Young Chinese captured by the Japanese.

A member of the Kung family, a Nation[...] photographed (centre) with Japanese officer[...] his home. 'Matsuaka agreed with these ideas [...] cited the situation in China as an example. Ch[...] Kai-shek, with whom he was in personal to[...] who knew him and trusted him, was gr[...] alarmed as to the further increase of the influ[...] of the Red Army in China.' (*Japan's Decisi[...] Surrender*, by R. J. Butow)

二十九年八月二十日亜聖殿前攝影

V   **Peasant Revolt**

`he ruthless economic exploitation and political oppression `the peasants by the landlord class forced them into numerous `risings against its rule . . . It was the class struggles of the `asants, the peasant uprisings and peasant wars that constit- `ed the real motive force of historical development in Chinese `idal society.' (The CCP and the Chinese Revolution)

`Without the poor peasants there would be no revolution. The `isses have potentially an inexhaustable enthusiam for social- `n and the poor peasants have always been the main force in `e bitter fight in the countryside.'
`he CCP and the Chinese Revolution)

The English word 'peasant' is a misleading term to apply to the Chinese farmer. In China, as in most parts of the world, peasants and farmers are not distinguished by different words. *Nung*, the classical word, means simply one who cultivates the soil, whether on a large or small scale. In more modern times the word for the rural population, and that which they themselves use, is *Lao Pai Hsing*, literally 'the old hundred surnames', because it is commonly (although inaccurately) said that there are only one hundred surnames in use among the Chinese people; hence, *Lao Pai Hsing* means 'the people'. It does not denote farmers or workmen, but would be best translated by the English words 'common people'. In popular speech it stands in opposition to the class of 'gentry', who were landowners but most of whom did not manage nor reside on their land. The rural masses, eighty per cent of the Chinese people—whom we call the peasants—are in their own eyes simply the majority of the common people.

To-day this majority is classified by the Chinese Communist Party into three categories, 'rich, middle, and poor peasants'. That is to say, the present population is described in terms which applied to their social and economic status more than twenty years ago when the Communist Party came to power. 'Poor peasants', now the most honoured group, are of course no longer poor but enjoy the same somewhat improved standard of living as the other groups, with greater political influence and social prestige. The rural farming population as a whole is now placed at the top of the social and political scale. The nation is exhorted to learn from the peasants; urban youth and professional men are sent to the countryside for longer or shorter periods to serve the rural population with their skills and to learn proletarian outlooks and ways of thought from the peasants among whom they live and work. It is a complete reversal of previous attitudes and views. Formerly the dearest, but generally unattainable, ambition of the peasant was to get off the land into some city occupation in which he could become literate and, far-off hope, qualify for competition in the public service examinations, so becoming one of the scholar gentry. To-day the urban scion of such a gentry family is sent back to the land to become a peasant farmer on a commune; this is not a degradation, nor a punishment, but is intended as an ennobling experience, a cleansing of the class contamination he has inherited.

The peasant is no longer left in illiterate ignorance; a vast scheme of rural education operates. Literacy is within reach of every child, and few indeed fail to attain it. The emphasis placed on the high value of the rural population and the consistent and far-reaching programmes to raise their educational level, care for their health and improve their living conditions are proof of the reality behind the policy of treating the peasants as the basic foundation of the state and the most important class within it. They also, by making rural life less harsh and more satisfying, do something to arrest the trend to migrate to the cities that is found the whole world over, and which is also a problem in China. The rural farming population forms the majority in China; it was also a class much oppressed and often grossly exploited under the former régime. Mao Tse-tung found the peasants of South China fertile soil for revolutionary activity and propaganda thirty and forty years ago. The view that peasants, particularly the landless labourers or those who owned only tiny plots insufficient for subsistence, were the real revolutionary class, the people to man the guerrilla armies and devote their lives to the cause, was formed and confirmed in the twenty-two year war which preceded the Communist victory in 1949. It is also now claimed that the peasants have always been a revolutionary class, and that the history of China, if properly interpreted, reveals this class war as its recurrent theme.

This view can be substantiated, in certain respects, by any study of Chinese history. From very ancient times the view that the people must be treated with justice and ruled with benevolence was expressed by philosophers and political thinkers, if far more rarely followed by kings. The classical age provides the example of a minister warning his reckless master that 'the people are like the waters, dam them up, and the dam will burst; the victims of the flood will be many'. He paid no attention, and the predicted calamity occurred. Mencius, the later follower of Confucius in the third century BC sanctified the right of rebellion when he said that 'he had heard of the execution of the criminal Chou, but not of the murder of a prince by his minister'. This referred to the slaying of the last king of Shang by his conqueror, the founder of the Chou kingdom. It has been cited ever since as justification for revolt against an evil ruler. Mencius also described the people (that is, the peasantry) as the 'base of the kingdom', meaning its essential foundation. Many later examples show that intelligent men of the ruling classes recognised the importance of the peasants, and decried the oppression to which they were so often subjected. They tried to cure the social evil by preaching a higher morality to the rulers, rather than seeking an economic or political solution. But the peasants, driven beyond a certain point sought solutions for their condition by revolt.

The modern Chinese interpretation, therefore, examines the great peasant rebellions of the past, and seeks to analyse their social aims and assess their revolutionary value. Some of the greatest of these revolts, the Red Eyebrows and Yellow Turbans of the Han period (first and third centuries AD), the great rebellion at the end of the Tang dynasty (ninth century AD), the rebellion which caused the fall of the Ming in 1644, and the Taiping Rebellion of the mid-nineteenth century, are seen as major class struggles against the gentry and imperial governments. Although these struggles either fatally weakened or overturned dynasties, they failed to achieve their full purpose because of the ambitions of their leaders, corrupted by power and lacking a firm ideological motivation. The Chinese people, it is now declared, have a very old—perhaps the oldest—revolutionary tradition, far more extensive in its operations than the local and small scale revolts of the European Middle Ages, far older than the revolutionary tradition dating from late eighteenth century France. Far from remaining the passive victims of class exploitation until modern times, the Chinese peasants, illiterate and ideologically untrained though they were, had a continuing tradition of subversive thinking and active rebellion whenever circumstances gave them the chance.

There can be no doubt that this new interpretation, differing profoundly from the traditional view, explains much, and has much validity; but it still leaves some problems unsolved and questions unanswered. The orthodox historians of the past attributed the revolts by the peasants to misgovernment by a declining dynasty (here the Communists are in full agreement) but saw this misrule as a consequence of the lack of virtue of the rulers, their failure to follow the precepts of Confucian morality and statecraft. They made no mention of economic causes, nor of social pressures. They also saw the leaders of the revolts as ambitious and wicked men seeking only to gain the throne for themselves. The contemporary historian seeks to discover the class origin of these leaders, and if it appears that they were malcontent and dissatisfied members of the ruling class (as was often the case), their subsequent failure to establish a better and juster society is adequately explained; lacking revolutionary origin and motivation, when they achieved success they must revert to the outlook and aims of the class from which they sprang. Such leaders as were genuinely of peasant or poor worker origin are seen too often as betrayed and supplanted by ambitious supporters of the wrong social origin.

There are some difficulties about this interpretation. Chu Yüan-chang, who founded the Ming dynasty in 1398 AD, came from the lowest social class; a famine refugee, who had been sold to a Buddhist monastery by his starving parents, he turned first bandit and then rebel, and led the great revolt which drove the Mongols out of China. He ruled as autocratic emperor for many years. Efficient and authoritarian and a great restorer of the Chinese system of government, he was still almost illiterate and subject to violent tempers during which he acted with arbitrary cruelty. This then, is the outstanding example of the successful poor man who led a great peasant revolt. He had not the benefit of education and could not aspire to any ideology.

It would seem that many of his less successful predecessors and, his two most famous successors—the leader of the rebellion which overturned the Ming, and the Heavenly King of the Taipings—had similar ambitions, and would have established similar régimes had they succeeded in consolidating their early victories. Whatever the vague hopes for a better life which inspired the mass of the followers, the leaders had no other aim than to displace the ruling dynasty and govern in its place, using the same system but one rejuvenated and staffed with their own followers. It was because this was the result of the great rebellions, whether successful or not (the dynasty usually fell before long), that the old social system and form of government always prevailed in the end. The illiterate soldiers who led the rebels had to rely on scholar gentry who joined them when the imperial cause seemed lost; they reconstructed the old system, and justified it by claiming that it would work well and benevolently under a new vigorous ruler.

If the results of peasant revolt were disappointing both to the followers and to their modern chroniclers, the causes and methods of revolt provide a more satisfactory revolutionary tradition. The Chinese peasantry have from immemorial times had a strong tradition of secret co-operation and organisation. Rural secret societies have persisted since the Han dynasty, and quite possibly are still older. They were organised to resist landlord and official extortions, sometimes by passive means, sometimes by open revolt.

If the latter method was used on a small scale, the distant Court would often send an officer to enquire into the source of the disorder, trace it to the misrule of the local official, have him dismissed —and executed—and pacify the people with assurances and promises of reform. The Court was rarely willing to aggravate disorder by wholesale repression, and feared the power of the greater secret societies, which had often infiltrated its own armed forces. The danger of such intervention by the Court was a potent check on the local officials, and a source of power to the secret societies. The introduction of modern arms gave the preponderance of power to the official side, and thus weakened the strength of peasant resistance to oppression. Man to man with sword and spear, Jack was as good as his master; but when faced by a soldier with a rifle the peasant was the certain loser.

The secret societies were inspired and co-ordinated by the adoption of some esoteric creed, usually that of a Buddhist sect or a Taoist cult; these creeds promised their followers divine protection (sometimes this included immunity from death in battle), paradise hereafter, and more precisely a better world here below. They had, in fact, a primitive form of revolutionary ideology, but in the modern view it was insufficiently thought out, resting on superstition and consequently ignoring the real economic and social forces behind revolt. Dr Sun Yat-sen, leader of the republican movement which finally dethroned the Manchu dynasty in 1912, was a member of one of the major societies and relied on secret society support for many years. It is significant that all his revolts failed; the succesful revolt at Wuhan in the centre of China was organised by revolutionaries who had infiltrated the army as soldiers and low-ranking officers. They rejected—or rather, did not rely upon—secret society support. When the local situation was very bad the secret societies could mobilise large numbers far in excess of the local governmental forces. Hence they always had early success. But they usually lacked organisation on a really wide scale. When they sought to extend their operations beyond their area of origin, they met with distrust and often opposition from the people, who feared to see their homes and farms plundered by an 'alien' army from another province. Thus, the secret society was most effective as a clandestine local opposition which inspired fear in the officials and landlords, restrained their exactions, and threatened disorder; this threat was more effective than the outbreak of revolt would have proved to be.

It has also been observed that the revolutionary rebel armies which sustained the greater revolts were made up not mainly of peasants, but of landless men, transport coolies (illpaid and grossly oppressed) and others who had no hope of better times in the exisiting social order and could only profit by rebellion and plunder. Peasants were not usually willing to serve far from home; they had their farms, and the landlords had fled. The landless labourers, charcoal burners from the mountains, porters, boatmen and the coolies of large cities, lived on a bare subsistence, had no property, no local attachment, and would follow any leader who gave them pay, loot and the chance to rise in his service. Thus, the Chinese revolutionary tradition is not quite what the Communists claim it to be, but it is also still further from what the orthodox historians of the past supposed it to be.

Non-Communist Chinese historians have said that Mao Tse-tung led the last and greatest peasant rebellion; he gave it new tactics and a long-term strategy, inspired it with a modern ideology instead of ancient superstitions, and above all constructed within the movement a hard core organisation of dedicated and instructed followers —the Communist Party—which could co-ordinate and administer. He sought to consolidate base areas won from the enemy, unlike so many rebellions of the past which roved the country from province to province and left no holding forces behind. They had all aimed at a quick march to the imperial capital and the dethronement of the dynasty. After early failures, the Communists avoided attacking large cities, and never struck at the capital until victory was already in their grasp. They promised land to the landless, they expropriated landlords, executed oppressive officials, and in other ways fulfilled the dreams and avenged the wrongs which the peasants felt most deeply. Communism as a doctrine was not preached to those who could not have understood it; its simpler economic programme made great appeal, its wider purpose was not then stressed. Thus, it is argued, Mao took the ancient Chinese peasant tradition of rebellion, modernised it, and gave it leadership which did not aim simply at the seizure of power within the old context, but planned a new society. These new motives altered the prospect of peasant revolt from ultimate failure to final victory. The Chinese Communist Party won power through peasant support, not by revolutionary action in large cities. This is the historical fact which so sharply distinguishes the Chinese and the Russian Communist Revolutions, and perhaps lies at the root of their subsequent antagonism.

Since the régime was originally built upon the outcome of a great peasant revolt, it is natural that the support of the peasants is still vital to it. The land reform programmes ending in the establishment of communes are by far the most sweeping and drastic changes in the economic and social system that the régime has carried out. In comparison the treatment of urban classes and the urban economy is moderate, and the political revolution, still essentially based on the policy of centralisation, can be seen as a modern form of the imperial régime without its personal characteristics and ceremonial glamour. The people, as Mencius observed, are the base. The peasantry, the old hundred surnames, form the majority of the Chinese people. The state must be built on this base, and the reformation of the economic and social standing of the peasantry is the essential policy for a new type of state. The real Chinese revolution has been the transformation of the rural economy and social system, a transformation which cannot now be reversed.

The recent Cultural Revolution can be seen, at least in one dominant aspect, as an attempt to introduce and insist upon peasant values in the entire nation. Learn from the people; send the urban folk back to the communes, make the professional experts, doctors and engineers, leave their hospitals, laboratories and universities to dwell among the people and give them the direct benefit of their learning, whilst themselves undergoing a similar education from their rural hosts. The Communist Party itself was regarded as infected, almost corrupted, by long urban association, and thus a prey to the type of 'revisionism' which marks the Russian Communist Party (always so urban in origin and make up). It had to be almost completely purged and reorganised in order to make it once more an organ of the people—the rural majority.

The people, peasants to the Western world, are now the favoured class, and to be a peasant, still better a 'poor peasant', is to be one of the élite. This is perhaps an unexpected, and possibly unfortunate result of the glorification of the peasant and his revolutionary consciousness. There are no longer any true 'poor peasants', since this type of miserable poverty was abolished by the régime itself. Those who were 'poor peasants', are now men of advancing years. Are their sons also 'poor peasants'? If they are to be so classed, then we are witnessing the beginning of a new hereditary social class, with status above those of other classes. This is not the avowed aim of the Chinese Communist Party, but unless the categories of peasants drawn up in pre-Communist times are now treated as an historical phenomenon and not as a continuing social reality, this could be the unintended but effective result.

The country bumpkin and the city slicker is not a Maoist antithesis. For Mao and his followers it is the peasantry who must be the chief inheritors of revolutionary power—their power; industry and the cities must not be the winners who take all. They resist urbanisation which they see as a major failure in the Western way of life. *Nung*, the common people of the countryside who comprise eighty per cent of China's population, with their fewer city brothers, were to establish 'the people's democratic dictatorship'. 'Arouse the masses of the people; that is, unite the working class, the peasantry, the urban *petit bourgeoisie*, form the domestic united front under the leadership of the working class—based on the alliance of workers and peasants. . . .

'Chiang Kai-shek betrayed Sun Yat-sen and used the dictatorship of the bureaucrat *bourgeoisie* and the landlord class as an instrument for suppressing the common people of China. This counter-revolutionary leadership was enforced for twenty-two years and has only now been overthrown by the common people under our leadership,' wrote Mao in 1949 in *The People's Democratic Dictatorship*.

On this statement to the infant People's Republic the whole of the new China's agricultural, educational, cultural and social life was to be based; but there were to be struggles and failures, and the Cultural Revolution (its full title is the Great Proletarian Cultural Revolution) was needed as a spectacular reaffirmation of purpose at a time when, after nearly twenty years of consolidating power, Party leaders saw *bourgeois*, bureaucratic and 'revisionist' influences eroding that democratic dictatorship. In spite of the success of the agricultural policies, the masses may be in danger of losing their heritage after their centuries-old struggle.

The whole land reform plan was completed by the end of 1952. Many of the landed gentry remained alive but with their power and influence greatly diminished; the old order had changed irrevocably. The first stage of rural re-organisation took the form of mutual aid teams, followed by agricultural co-operatives based on the principle of property amalgamation. Later higher, fully socialised co-operatives evolved, which led to the establishment of communes in 1958— more it is said by pressure of demands from below than from the leadership. The communes were to control not just agriculture but local industry, commerce and primary education. Mao quickly realised the significance of peasant interest in this commune principle and warmly supported it. Today, after considerable administrative and organisational changes, the communes are universally accepted and join together for larger projects such as irrigation or afforestation schemes. A commune groups together several villages, each maintaining some identity and independence; each village is a 'work brigade' divided into some ten to fifteen 'work teams' of forty or fifty households each. There are now about 75 000 communes whose sizes vary from 2 000 to 50 000 acres according to the productivity of the area.

Population ranges from 20 000 to 50 000. Each work team elects a small committee which sends representatives to a Brigade Committee that, in turn, elects members to the Commune Council.

One of the major definitive statements of the Cultural Revolution, the Central Committee's Decision of 8 August 1966 made clear the role of the peasants and in September that same year Marshall Lin

Piao, then Mao's heir apparent, hit the headlines with a call to world revolution, but Lin was only restating Marxist-Maoist theories, and the need for the common people to be as strenuously vigilant as ever. 'The masses of workers, peasants and soldiers under the leadership of the CCP have always been the main force of the revolution in our country. Today they are the main force of the Socialist régime and also the main force of the great proletarian revolution.'

This amalgam of peasant masses and the proletariat is the key to success in all economic developments. Agriculture is to serve industry, feeding and helping to clothe the workers. Industry must be equally responsible to and for the peasantry. 'We must on no account regard industry and agriculture, Socialist industrialisation and the Socialist transformation of agriculture, as two separate and isolated things and on no account must we emphasise one and play down the other,' declared Mao's directive in 1955, *On the Question of Agricultural Co-operation*. The same order of priorities was made clear at the tenth plenary session of the Central Committee in 1962.

The exhortation 'In agriculture learn from Tachai' has been made millions of times. One of the most familiar faces to the Chinese and to readers of China's Foreign Language Press publications, is that of Comrade Chen Yung-kwei with his strong features, weathered skin and wide smile, towel wrapped peasant-style round his head. This man, secretary of a brigade in the Tachai commune, North China, is the model of all model workers. It is his determination, his enterprise, stemming from his 'correct political line', that have led his little band to transform the wilderness and solitary places of his arid native Shensi commune. 'Situated at the foot of the Tachai Mountains Tachai is a production brigade of the Tachai People's Commune in Shansi Province. It consists of 83 households with a population of 380 and owns about 166 acres of arable land. Before Liberation Tachai was a village of 60 households and the poor and lower middle peasants accounted for 70 per cent of the population. They toiled for the landlord as casual labourers subject to hunger and cold. After agricultural co-operation in 1958 Tachai was still faced with natural disadvantages of gullies, ridges and soil erosion. . . .

'Acting according to Chairman Mao's teaching, "from the masses to the masses" they held an extensive debate and decided to develop the spirit of the old man who removed the mountains and remake nature with their own hands. The poor and lower middle peasants worked out a ten-year plan to transform the ridges, gullies and slopes into arable land. It was very successful. Before Liberation the average yield per mou never exceeded 100 catties; by 1967 it had leapt to over 900 catties. In addition to increase in grain output there was a corresponding growth in forestry, stock breeding and side-occupations.'

The whole Tachai concept is of immense importance, for it is the Tachais, above all, that are the life blood, the core, of the body politic and economic alike. After his return from a long stay on a Shensi commune Jan Myrdal explained in a paper to the Chicago China Conference in 1966: 'As the peasants of Liu Ling village said, "Nothing comes from heaven, everything comes from work". Their work. Grain production that year had been 327 000 points. The state grain tax had been 24 000 pounds and 22 000 pounds has been sold to the state. And on these 46 000 pounds (together with the equivalent deliveries from 11 of the other villages) rests not only the whole Chinese state with armies and atomic weapons and universities and diplomats and national monuments, but also the new industrial development. If China is to survive and develop, these deliveries must increase.'

And increase they did, as John Gittings reported in 1972 for the *Far Eastern Economic Review*: 'Since the Cultural Revolution harvests have increased by about ten per cent; granaries are full and shops well-stocked. Yields are steadily rising, prices of fertilisers and farm machinery are falling by about 15 per cent.'

One of the more remarkable records of peasants' indefatigable efforts literally to remove mountains, comes from Central China's Honan Province—the building of the Red Flag Canal. 'For long years, over one-half of the country's manpower was spent getting water from dozens of li away by crossing hills. Starting from 1960, the people of Linhsein worked hard for ten years and finally diverted water from the Changha River in neighbouring Shansi Province to the country.' Evident everywhere is the back-breaking labour of millions of peasants, the major contribution of China's economic and social development.

Not only have purely agricultural works to be undertaken; rural areas must be industrialised in all possible ways. One Chinese Communist ideal is a modest version of the Renaissance man: till the soil, keep accounts, weave cloth, build and repair machines, run small factories, provide hydro-electric stations, modern communications—even modern gadgets—for the commune. Professor Joseph Needham, Cambridge scientist and sinologist, commented in 1971 on the many successful small industries which he saw in the countryside. But complete rural independence is clearly impossible and undesirable. Heavy industry must play a major role in rural development. 'Agriculture is the foundation', the cities were reminded constantly and the following appeared in *Ta hung Pao* in 1972: 'The heavy industries took it upon themselves to make contributions to farm mechanisation and to increase output and varieties in the spirit of self-reliance and hard struggle. The result is more tractors, more walking-tractors, more internal combustion engines, more motors for farm machinery and more spare parts for these and others.'

The very success of agricultural industrialisation in both city and village has produced divisive debate at the topmost level and may have been a major factor in Lin Piao's downfall. Investment in agritural mechanisation meant smaller investment in more advanced industrial sectors, which were essential to what the military leaders saw as a vital expansion and modernisation of the country's defence system.

Mao's first published work was an article in his student days urging more attention to physical education and extolling its various health-giving qualities. Not surprisingly, therefore, health services have been stressed from the days of the first Chinese soviets. The country-side was to have its own type of medical services and though equipment and facilities were obviously to be simple, every effort was to be made to evolve services of the best possible quality. Gradually, from 1949 onwards, clinics were provided in most villages, mobile services for more remote areas and health education and preventive medicine were to be widely developed. When the Cultural Revolution brought its root-and-branch reorganisation of the education system, medical training was metamorphosed with the stress very much on services in rural areas. Thousands of medical assistants and nurses were given crash training courses of various lengths, and local skills in traditional medicine—especially herbal medicine—were called on, so that by the early 1970s health services of one kind or another had multiplied greatly. *China Pictorial* reported in 1970: 'Changshu County, Kiangsu, has built a completely new rural medical and health network encompassing the whole county. This includes a hospital of twenty to thirty simple hospital beds with twenty medical workers for each commune to take care of prevention and treatment of disease; a clinic for every production brigade with one or two barefoot doctors, a midwife and a medical worker transferred there from a higher level; and a health worker in every production team who is in charge of preventive work exclusively.'

On their return from visits to China, many Western doctors and social workers have written about the expanding rural health services, including Dr S. B. Rifkin of London who visited China in 1971: 'China is making significant progress in efforts to provide its people with practical—and unique—health services . . . which concentrate on the essential needs of the people. The service relies on this and on medical auxiliaries who travel the hinterland with little more than a first-aid box and the Thoughts of Mao Tse-tung. Depending on a system by which they can refer serious cases to highly-trained medical staff, on periodic visits from doctors attached to mobile medical teams, on preventive medical techniques and the full confidence of their patients, the auxiliaries are the core of a scheme that is trying to give China's rural population some kind of medical treatment. . . . The lynch-pin of the system is "the barefoot doctor" . . . poor and lower middle class peasants . . . whose work is supported not only by such people as traditional medical assistants, nurses, midwives and laboratory technicians, but also by thousands of public health workers . . . who, to quote one report from Yenchiang County, "learn to prevent and treat minor injuries and diseases, administer preventive shots and perform the four skills of tourniquet, bandaging, fixing and moving". They also know some acupuncture techniques.'[1]

'The serious problem is the education of the peasants. . . . The people's capacity for learning is profound.' For Mao these truths are as self-evident today as they were in the days of ninety per cent peasant illiteracy, but the emphasis is different. After twenty years of strenuous educational effort and much success Mao saw 'embourgeoisement' setting in—a drift from the country, from rural to urban ideas and ideals, from the common people to a new élite; to restore Marxist-Leninist fervour, came the significantly and accurately named Great Proletarian Cultural Revolution. One of Mao's directives during the Cultural Revolution emphasised: 'In carrying out the Proletarian Cultural Revolution in education it is essential to have working class leadership; it is essential for the masses of workers to take part. . . . In the countryside the schools must be managed by the poor and lower middle peasants . . . the most reliable ally of the working class. . . . It is essential to shorten the length of schooling, revolutionise education and put proletarian politics in command. Students should be selected from workers and peasants with practical experience and they should return to production [in factory or commune] after a few years' study.'

Workers and peasants by the thousands (along with men of the People's Liberation Army) entered educational institutions. They spread Mao's directives exhorting students to remember the debts owed to the revolutionary common people of the past, to revise their thinking so that they allied themselves closely with workers and peasants who were, indeed, the parents of many bright young students who were coming perilously near to rejecting their common-people heritage.

Not only did peasants take an active part in the management of village schools, syllabuses were oriented towards the practicalities of the country children's everyday life and to Marxism-Leninism and Mao Tsetung Thought. 'Syllabuses are decided on by the Revolutionary Committee in charge of the school. At a Kiangsi primary school it consisted of two pupils, four teachers and a local peasant . . . they ensure the integration of the school into the local community. A maths lesson brought home to us how . . . a subject has an important role in teaching "Communist morality". Some of the sums the eight year olds were working at compared the landlord's holdings and income with those of the peasants in the pre-liberation era; others compared pre- and post-Cultural Revolution statistics with the teacher, pointing out that only when the workers took control from "the capitalist leaders" were such advances possible.'[2]

Adults, too, should study hard and note the third of the three great revolutionary movements: 'Peking workers and peasants on the outskirts . . . act in line with Chairman Mao's teaching, "Class struggle, the struggle for production and scientific experiment are the three great revolutionary movements for building a mighty Socialist country" . . . In a vigorous campaign for technical innovations last year Peking workers put more than 10 000 innovations into effect . . .'.[3]

Like the old man who removed the mountain in ancient legend and in Mao's most-read article, the peasants and workers can accomplish near-miracles.

Above all, country people, like city dwellers, should study politics, Marxism-Leninism and Mao Tsetung Thought, 'so that they may make progress ideologically [for] not to have a correct political point of view is like having no soul'. Since this is necessary not only for children in school but for all country workers, spare-time study classes are an accepted part of village life. A typical *People's Daily* account of such classes tells how the 'broad masses of Hopei province' set up various kinds of study classes taking 'fight self, repudiate revisionism' as their guiding principle. One of these, the revolutionary aunts' study class, discusses Chairman Mao's works collectively. It is important to note that classes were set up with the help of the People's Liberation Army which took part in such activities throughout the country during the Cultural Revolution and continues to do so, though probably with less vigour than before.

It was made clear that to carry out the Proletarian Cultural Revolution working class leadership was essential; it is also recognised that other classes must play their part; A proletarian education system cannot be self-generating; cross-fertilisation with the educated classes—the intellectuals and the artists—is necessary. Education and the arts, indeed, are to be a vital link between the classes on the way to the classless society. Distinctions disappear as one teaches the other to mutual advantage. 'We must have working intellectuals and intellectual workers', ran Mao's slogan along a Peking University wall.

A desolate gully before transformation, the old Tachai was a rocky hilly area with poor soil and unruly waters. Its land was spread out over these harsh gullies, ridges and hill-slopes.

Chen Yung-kwei, Chairman of the Tachai Branch of the CCP. 'The heroic Tachai people, full of vigour and enthusiasm, have indeed transformed their impoverished mountain village into a new socialist Tachai in line with Chairman Mao's instruction, "Be resolute, fear no sacrifice and surmount every difficulty to win victory".'

Civilian builders on the Haiho River project work to remove earth.

Apart from interplanting, the Tachai people have tried many other ways to extend and make full use of the arable land. Even vertical banks such as these have been utilised.

'They levelled 1 250 hilltops, opened 134 tun
with a total length of 24 kilometres, built
bridges totalling 6·5 kilometres long and dug
built 16 400 000 cubic metres of stone and ea
work, completely changing the appearance
nature . . . in a hard battle lasting a year and
months.' (*Red Banner Hungchi Canal*, F.L.P.)

...ested corn at Hsiatingchia village.

...rner of the new housing estate built by the
...nui People's Commune for its members in
...uburbs of Chengtu, Szechwan Province. The
...ment comprises twenty-one buildings includ-
...suites of rooms for whole families, a public
...urant, a health centre, a store, a tailoring
...p, a library, a kindergarten and other
...ities.

A new cottage on a commune in Shantung province.

This new commune primary school near Hangchow contains six classrooms, two laboratories, three activity rooms, a clinic, offices, three extra classrooms (kept in reserve to allow for growth), 240 children and a Chinese-made harmonium.

commune village has its own carpenters,
layers and often electricians, but industry is
needed to help with large projects in irrigation,
munications and electrification schemes as well
with the provision of heavy agricultural
pment.

The Hsinwu commune has experienced the growth of farm mechanisation in recent years. Tractors are used to do deep ploughing. 'The most urgent task facing the people of our country at present is to carry through the general policy of developing the national economy, with agriculture as the foundation and industry as the leading factor.' (Tenth plenary session of CCP, 1962)

Cheap to make, easy to handle and repair, the 'walking' tractor is a valuable asset to all communes. These are made in the Wuhan Walking Tractor Plant.

training of barefoot doctors of Yao nationality
their history of a lack of doctors and medicine.
dical auxiliaries travel the hinterland with
more than a first-aid box and the Thoughts
ao Tsetung, depending on a system by which
can refer serious cases to highly-trained
ical staff, on periodic visits from doctors
hed to mobile medical teams, on preventive
ical technique. . . . The auxiliaries are the
of a scheme that is trying to give China's rural
ulation some kind of medical treatment.'
S. B. Rifkin, *Far Eastern Economic Review*,
ch 1972)

A small machine tool factory in a commune. 'The
people themselves work in these factories scattered
all over the length and breadth of the land. It's
very important—why should people be "hayseeds"?
If you have in your commune several very nice
factories you can learn a lot. In the thirty-three
small factories in Wa-an in Hopei, employing
5 000 people, no less than 4 000 are *neng jen*, that
is, farmers, peasants, agriculturalists. In their spare
time they operate machines and become modern
people; they aren't stuck in the mud as their
ancestors were for so many centuries; they've got
all sorts of chances today.' (Professor Joseph
Needham, *China Now*, 1971)

'The poor and lower middle peasants on Peking's outskirts popularised a number of highly-effective plant hormones and high-yielding seed strains and carried out experiments in multiple cropping and inter-planting.' (*New China News*, 1972)

Commune agricultural science laboratory in Shantung.

worker staying in a primary school gives a
~~our course.~~ 'In the countryside the schools must
managed by the poor and lower middle
~~sants.~~ . . . It is essential to shorten the length
schooling, revolutionise education and put
~~letarian~~ politics in command. Students should
selected from workers and peasants with
~~ctical~~ experience and they should return to
~~duction~~ [in factory or commune] after a few
~~rs'~~ study.' (Mao Tse-tung, 1968)

'What will I be when I grow up?' (A verse in a
children's school reader.)
'When I grow up I will be a peasant,
    And I will build new villages for my motherland.
When I grow up I will make machines,
    And I will send them to the villages.
When I grow up I will join the army
    To protect our motherland and defeat our
enemies.
Workers, peasants and soldiers are very important,
very revolutionary,
    When we grow up we will be workers, peasants
and soldiers.'

'Ideological education is the key link to be grasped.' (Mao Tse-tung Directive) 'Virtually every foreign traveller to China has reported that it is now possible to ask a peasant a political question and expect an answer. It may simply be parotted from Radio Peking but at least the Chinese will not stand there dumbstruck as do peasants almost everywhere else in Asia.' (*Newsweek* 21 February 1972)

'Running study classes is a good method; you c arrive at a solution to many problems in th classes,' said Mao Tse-tung. Aunt Li, a p peasant in the old society, gives an account of I 'past sufferings and present happiness'. (*Ch Pictorial*)

ections from textbooks written by peasants in
eh-chin Brigade for use in a commune primary
ool. (*Peking Renmin Ribao*, 14 January 1969)

Several Arithmetical Questions
by
a poor peasant member, Chi Fu-ch'ing

airman Mao teaches us: 'Never forget class
iggle.' My family consisted of six persons before
liberation. I worked for the landlord as a hired
id, and was required to farm 15 mow of paddy
year and produce 620 catties of paddy per
w. The landlord, whose heart was more veno-
us than that of a viper and more vicious than
t of a wolf, thought of all conceivable ways to
loit us poor and lower-middle peasants. It was
eed that our wages were to be 8 piculs of rice
ear, but after deductions of all kinds we could
e only 6·5 piculs a year, which was not enough
the family. In the old society there were 13 of
in Hsi-ts'unpien who worked as hired hands
d 4 girls were sold as child-wives.

hen the sun rose and the east was red. Chairman
o led us in overthrowing the three mountains
l saved us from the sea of sorrow. We became
sters of the country and our lot has improved
adily. We must never forget the Communist
ty and Chairman Mao for our liberation and
piness. But renegade Liu Shao-ch'i tried to drag
onto the capitalist road and make us suffer again.
must struggle against him resolutely.

ckon the following:
Before the liberation, how many persons were
re in Hsi-ts'un-pien who worked as hired hands
l how many were sold as child-wives?
Poor peasant Chi Fu-ch'ing farmed 15 mow
paddy for the landlord and was required to
duce 620 catties of paddy per mow a year.
at was the total quantity of paddy Chi Fu-
ing produced a year?
The landlord paid Chi Fu-ch'ing only 6·5
uls of rice (one picul of rice being the equivalent
oo catties of paddy) in wages a year. How many
ties of paddy could Chi Fu-ch'ing have after
year's labour? How many catties of paddy
the landlord expropriate from him? What was
percentage of the total output that was
ropriated by the landlord? What was the
centage of the total output that Chi Fu-ch'ing
eived as wages after toiling for a whole year?

12   The Peasant and the Revolutionary Tradition

From the earliest times the Chinese view of empire was far remov
from any divine right of kings or the Lord's anointed. A ruler held
mandate only as long as he ruled the people to their reasona
satisfaction. About 300 BC Mencius justified the overthrow of a k
who outraged humanity, and Hsun Tzu, in the third century I
expanded on this: 'The government is there for the people not
the ruler; a bad ruler can be deposed.'

When a dynasty was failing it was the peasants who suffered m
as poets and historians recorded.

> The silk shared out in the Vermilion Hall
> Was woven by hands of poor women
> Women whose men were whipped in their own homes
> By tax collectors who took the silk to court,
> Behind those vermilion gates meat and wine go to waste
> While out on the road lie the bones of men frozen to death.
>
> (Tu Fu, AD 712–77

Lu Chih wrote about the hopeless conditions that existed: 'Wl
the peasant is ruined, he has to sell his field and his hut. If it happ
to be a good year, he may just be able to pay his debts. But no soo
has the harvest been brought in than the grain bins are empty aga
and contract in hand and sack on back, he has to go off and st
borrowing again. He has heavier and heavier interest to pay, a
soon has not got enough to eat. If there is a famine he falls into ut
ruin. Families disperse, parents separate, they seek to become slav
and no one will buy them . . .'

With such burdens and such a mandate for rebellion it is
surprising that China experienced many peasant uprisings, nor t
most Communist historians, as well as Mao Tse-tung, have p
great heed to these and tend to interpret their country's history
terms of peasant rebels versus the 'establishment' of their day. 'Fr
the first century AD to the tenth century . . . the large scale peas
revolts broke out. Memorable among these was the Green Wc
Army in AD 21 . . . which entered the capital in AD 23. Towa
the end of the Eastern Han Dynasty . . . new famines led to n
peasant revolts of which the most famous was that of the Yell
Turbans. Led by Chang Chao this great rising began in AD 184 .
and spread through eleven provinces. The landlords banded togetl
to suppress it . . . In 875 Huan Chao, a fairly prosperous s
merchant, put himself at the head of a rural revolt in Honan starti
a ten year peasant war unprecedented in scale which raged ove
great part of China. In 880 Huan Chao took the capital Sian . . .
T'ang emperor fled but was able to counter attack and drive Hua
to Shantung where he committed suicide . . . The peasant for
called the Red Turban Army swept over the north between 1
and 1359, and the lower reaches of the Yangtse were taken
boatmen engaged in transporting salt. In the river's middle reacl
the leader was a cloth pedlar . . . But none of these forces succeed
in overthrowing the Yuan dynasty . . . In 1635 thirteen rebel lead
met in Northern Honan. They won popular support . . . as they w
uncompromising to aristocrats, high officials and landlords, taki
their lives and distributing their property to the poor.'[1]

The peasants' resistance to the Opium War marauders at S
Yuan Li in 1841 is seen as a major struggle of the day, betrayed
the official class. An account by two British observers lends so

force to this interpretation. 'In May 1841 when British marauders sneaked into San Yuan Li near Canton, tens of thousands of peasants from 103 villages raised banners bearing the emblem *PING YING TUAN* ('Quell the British Corps'). The women and children supplied their menfolk with food and water. Despite desperate attempts to break out more than 200 British were killed or wounded. Finally Yi Shan (a Chinese general) sent men to San Yuan Li and by cajolery and threats forced the peasants to disperse. The struggle of the Ping Ying Tuan, the first heroic mass fight of the Chinese people in modern history against the foreign aggressors, stands out in sharp contrast to the corruption and impotence of the capitulators in the Ching government.'[2]

W. H. Hall and W. S. Bernard add a confirmatory footnote to this account: 'At length the Prefect arrived and assured the [British] General that the movement of these peasants was quite without the sanction or knowledge of the authorities and that he would immediately send off an officer of rank to see that they dispersed to their houses.'[3]

Peasant suffering from flood, famine, and drought increased each decade as population pressures diminished the amount of available land. G. B. Cressey says that in 1666 there were 5·24 mou of land per head, in 1766 this had shrunk to 4·07 and in 1872 to 2·49 mou per head.

In 1850, when the great Taiping Rebellion broke out in Central China, a number of fierce uprisings among the minority peoples, some in remoter areas, echoed the Taiping's wrath. 'The Ching soldiers were so afraid of the Nien peasant army that even the dust raised in the distance by their marching feet struck terror into them. Their force grew to 100 000 strong and reached the gates of Tientsin. But the Nien army failed to set up bases and its soldiers had no rest. The uprising finally failed.

'The struggle of the Miao people (in Kweichow) persisted for eighteen years shaking the Ching rule in the south-west provinces . . . The Huis of China's north-west suffered brutal oppression at the hands of Ching officials and rose repeatedly in revolt. A large-scale uprising broke out in 1862 and it was not until 1873 that the Hui insurgents were finally suppressed. A great multi-national revolt flared up in Sinkiang led by the Uighur people in 1864. All these uprisings of minority peoples went on side by side with the Taiping Revolution and from this common struggle is seen the community of interests of all nationalities in China.'

The turn of the century brought the Boxer Rebellion. This was shorter, less bloody and destructive than the Taiping, but far more familiar to and deplored by the West because of the rebel's attacks on Christian missionaries, and because of the much-publicised raising of the fifty-five days' siege of the Peking legations by some eight foreign armies. Their governments saw the subsequent sack of the city as fair retribution for Boxer atrocities. The Chinese today see the Boxer movement rather differently, as Chou En-lai has said: 'The Ho Tuan movement of 1900 was a demonstration of the Chinese people's resistance against imperialism; its heroic struggle was one of the foundation stones for the great victory of the Chinese people fifty years later.' Many Western historians record the injustices resulting from the concessions given to Westerners, for example,

G. B. Smyth in his article 'The Crisis in China': 'The position of equality with viceroys and governors given to the Bishops, and the equality of provincial judges . . . given to the various orders of priests, gave the Roman Catholics an influence of which the people had good reason to believe they would not be slow to avail themselves. In lawsuits between adherents and non-Christian people the latter had, they thought, no chance . . . there was a general complaint of the constant interference of the priests in litigation.'[4]

Inevitably excesses occurred; innocent blood was shed when the Boxers in their frustration set out to massacre the 'Western devils'. The posters and speeches made clear their fury and their intentions, and many innocent foreigners were to suffer with the guilty.

The main revolutionary ferment came from one level or another of the peasants, but the rebel armies of Taipings and Boxers recruited thousands from the strata above and below them, as well as displaced persons. 'Hung, a teacher and failed scholar, Yang, a charcoal burner, Feng, a village teacher, Chao, a poor peasant, Wei, a businessman and Shih, a rich peasant, were the Taiping leaders, but none belonged to the gentry class. Their first disciples were several thousand poor Hakka peasants, several hundred charcoal burners, thousands of mine-workers and a considerable number of former pirates who had been chased from the seas by foreign warships. There were even a few rich businessmen, peasants and learned people as well as deserters from the government and coolies from Canton who had lost their jobs as a result of the Opium War.'[5]

A contemporary observer in Kwantung commented in 1840 on the problem, for thousands of men supported their families by working as porters, some having worked at this occupation for generations. Of course, there were many Chinese at court, in country mansions, and later in the Western trading houses who unreservedly rejected the right to rebel; they demanded a place in society for everyone and everyone in his place. One of these was Tseng Kuo-fan, a scholar, landlord and military leader who finally defeated the Taipings after fifteen years of rebellion: 'Throughout history men have upheld this doctrine which expounds the pattern of men's relationships, of prince and subject, father and son, high and low, noble and humble, in an order that may no more be reversed than the position of cap and shoe . . . The Chinese Book of Odes and Book of History which for thousands of years have been our guides . . . are now used to sweep the floor with. This is a rebellion not only against the dynasty but the doctrine of the Sages. How can men of education endure to sit with their hands in their sleeves doing nothing?' Nationalist historians would favour such a line. Chiang Kai-shek strongly supports it, rejecting any concept of a glorious tradition of peasant risings. While firmly rejecting Chiang's extremist attitude many Communist historians, especially the older ones, modify the more enthusiastic claims for peasant leadership, stressing the contributions which came from other classes and also, in the ranks, from the *lumpenproletariat*. In 1964 Sun Tso-min wrote: 'In the past there appeared [in] studies by some comrades of the history of the peasant wars, unhistorical tendencies in the exaggeration of the [revolutionary] consciousness of the peasant rebel leaders.'

A further consideration for modern Chinese historians is Marx's highly sceptical attitude to peasant revolutionary capacity, based on his study of European rural traditions. 'The peasantry', said Engels, 'try to roll back the wheel of history', and though he admired 'peasant revolutionary energy and resolution' he also feared their narrow-mindedness and seemed not to envisage a predominantly peasant revolution.

When not in open rebellion, China's oppressed or exploited classes across the whole social spectrum had banded together in those secret societies which exercised a very strong influence, checking the excesses of imperial officials, war-lords or landlords. When the Taipings and Boxers failed and the scholar-led reform movements foundered, many secret societies began to support Sun Yat-sen. One of the most important was the peasant society, Ko Lao Hui. General Chu Teh described his initiation to Agnes Smedly: 'It wasn't long before they invited him to join the Ko Lao Hui. His initiation took place before many soldier members who gathered at an isolated temple in the hills. There he went through the ancient ritual which including much kowtowing and drinking the blood oath of brotherhood. First Chu Teh and the members giving the oath cut a vein in their wrists and allowed a few drops of their blood to fall into a bowl of wine. The bowl was then passed round and each of the principals drank a little. As this was done Chu pledged deathless loyalty to the society's principles. He then learned the signs and passwords by which members can, to the present day, identify one another anywhere.'[6]

In her book *Struggle for the New China*, Sun Yat-sen's widow, Soong Ching-ling discusses his concern for peasant suffering and his determination to win the peasants to his revolutionary cause. But for all his concern, Sun, in common with his revolutionary predecessors, failed to grasp the main requisites for peasant power, as the contemporary Communist historian, Liu Kwei-wu says, 'The programme of the Tung Meng Hui revolutionary league not only had the support of the *bourgeoisie* but was also welcomed by the masses of the people. The organisation became a mighty force pushing forward the democratic revolution. Its land programme, however, failed to mention the necessity to mobilise the masses of the peasants, and thus reduce its slogans for the solution of the land problem to mere talk.

'Yet the founding of the *bourgeois* political party, the Tung Meng Hui, pushed the Chinese revolution ahead. The organisation . . . launched many uprisings. These, however, were still revolts of the few. They did not have the support of the masses because the leaders, who feared the workers and peasants, neither mobilised the masses nor did patient work to organise them. As a result the revolts were suppressed.'[7]

Mao was not to make the same mistake. Peasant rebels were no longer to be roving bands but a disciplined guerrilla force operating from established bases. And, most important, *bourgeois* intellectuals were to identify their destiny with that of the common people. From the time of writing his now famous *Report on the Peasant Movement in Hunan* in 1927 up to and after the Cultural Revolution, Mao was to proclaim this line in writing, speech and action. The task was Herculean.

In 1972 the Writing Group of the Yunan Communist Party analysed the situation during the late 1920s and 1930s. 'The feudal landlord class was the main social base of imperialist rule in China, while the peasants were the main force of the revolution. To lead the revolution to victory the proletariat had to arm the peasants, carry out the land revolution and build solid revolutionary bases in the countryside. "In semi-colonialist China", said Mao, "the establishment and expansion of the Red Army . . . and the Red areas is the highest form of peasant struggle . . .". Whether or not to build revolutionary base areas was a major question of principle over which Chairman Mao waged repeated struggles against "left" and right opportunist lines. How could the land revolution be carried out without establishing rural revolutionary bases? By mobilising the masses of peasants to take part in the land revolution in accordance with Chairman Mao's line we succeeded in building the Red Army . . . established revolutionary base areas from scratch and expanded those.'

Nor was Mao to make Sun's mistake of letting land reform slogans be 'reduced to mere talk'. In the Kiangsi soviets in the early 1930s the process of redistributing land and reducing interest rates got well under way. A vast reservoir of emotion was opened up—and with it a vast array of problems.

After generations of stored up bitterness the peasants inevitably sought revenge on their oppressors. But from the start Mao set his face against wanton destruction and excess; these could only alienate millions of potential supporters. 'Pay great attention', he said, 'to winning over the intermediate classes and avoid blind action—acts of house burning, the practice of shooting deserters and inflicting corporal punishment.' He sought 'education not slaughter, persuasion not liquidation'—not that the greedy and more vicious landlords were allowed to escape unscathed, by any means.

But the forces pitted against the reforms and against the young soviets were immense—landlords and their dependents, industrialists and merchants, foreign financial interests, and the fanatically anti-Red Chiang Kai-shek at the head of his vast armies. 'Positive action', he said in 1934, 'will be taken to prepare the armed forces to mop up the remnants of the Red bandits.'

For all their revolutionary potential, the peasant masses had to be roused from their lethargy and despair. At first very little could be offered: 'The masses failed completely to understand what the Red Army was. It was even attacked as a bandit gang and had no support from the masses. We had great difficulty in finding encampments, carrying on military operations and securing information. We had to march across snow-covered, icy mountains closely pursued by the enemy. We sometimes covered thirty miles in a single day. Our sufferings increased . . . Fortunately, we are inured to hardships. Furthermore all alike share the same hardships; everybody from the army commander down to the cook lives on daily fare worth five cents, apart from grain.'[8] Traditionally, the poor peasant's place was the lowest on the scale; more often than not he was some homeless wretch in a war-lord's army, underpaid, underfed, out to grab what he could in his short span. 'Good iron does not become a nail, a good man does not become a soldier' ran the Chinese proverb but Mao and Chu Teh were to change such material—poor peasants, *lumpenproletariat*—into fighting men by promises of fair dealing, by political education, and amazingly in the China of those days, by kindness. Over and over again the message is repeated: 'Our army must become one with the people so that they see it as their own army. Such an army will be invincible.' Some of the practical results of this policy were summed up crisply in the famous eight rules of the Red Army.

1. Speak politely; 2. Pay fairly for what you buy; 3. Return anything you borrow; 4. Pay for everything you damage; 5. Don't strike or swear at people; 6. Don't damage crops; 7. Don't take liberties with women; 8. Don't ill-treat captives.

But revolutionary fervour was not enough. Political education could not be carried out, nor military training mastered by the illiterate. Agnes Smedly records General Chu Teh's story of the literacy campaigns of the 1930s and 1940s. 'The Cultural Department of the Soviets turned temples into free primary schools for poor children. At night when the children moved out adult illiterates came in. . . . There were few teachers, little paper and no blackboards . . . Thus began what General Chu called "the greatest study movement in Chinese history", a movement reflected in slogans painted on walls, cliffs, and even the trunks of trees: "Learn, learn and learn again! . . . Study until the light fails! . . . Study as you plough . . . Study by the reflected light of snow!"'

'In those days the army had to do almost everything. Every man in its ranks able to impart knowledge spent any leisure moment he might have in teaching the peasants. . . . Primary school teachers who announced the opening of a school for children in some temple would appear at the stipulated time to find almost the entire village, from old grandfathers to mothers with babies at their breasts, sitting side by side with their children on the school benches and spilling into the temple courtyards.'

Mao talked of his recruits in the early days: 'The proportion of vagabond elements is large and there are great masses of vagabonds in China. Some want to expand the army by recruiting almost anyone. But we must intensify education to counter the vagabond outlook, draw active workers into the ranks of the army to change its composition and deepen agricultural reform. We must not have a roving bandit army.'

Mao and his supporters, military and civil alike, realised that sooner or later they would be defeated unless they increased their forces and armed them better. 'Power grows out of the barrel of a gun' and Chiang Kai-shek had far more guns—as the peasant army found after its gallant attempt under the leadership of Chou En-lai to take and hold the city of Nanchang, Kiangsi Province, in July and August 1927. With the remnants of their ragged forces they withdrew to join Mao in the wild Chingkang Mountains on the borders of Kiangsi and Hunan. Soon after, Chu Teh and his men broke through the Kuomintang blockade to join them and lay the foundations for the People's War that was to last some twenty years.

'Despite its defeat the Nanchang Uprising had a great historic significance, for it marked the birth of the Chinese People's Army an army under the sole leadership of the CCP and whole-heartedly dedicated to the cause of the People's revolution. A new historical epoch thus began for the revolutionary struggle.'[9]

Given time the Red Army could turn defeat into final victory.

But it had to live off the land and this was possible only if the peasants and the countryfolk accepted and supported them. This in turn was possible only if all were aware, soldiers and peasants alike, of what they were seeking. There must be a firm political base. 'We must have a CCP organisation for the widespread ideological work of remoulding the *bourgeois* outlook and strengthening the proletarian leadership,' insisted Mao. Like Cromwell's Ironsides they were to know what they fought for and love what they knew. One of the strongest affirmations of the way the peasant's sense of their mission developed is found in a 'Proclamation of the Peasants of the Border Region' (in Northern China) made many years later when the revolution was nearing victory. 'The poor and hired peasants should lead because they make up 50–70 per cent of the population . . . and work hardest all the year long. They plant the land, they build the buildings, they weave the cloth but they never have enough food to eat, a roof to sleep under or clothes to wear. Their life is most bitter . . . From birth they are a revolutionary class. Inevitably they are the leaders of the *fanshen* movement. This is determined by life itself.' William Hinton, the American agricultural advisor and teacher working in China during the final land reforms, vividly explains the significance of *fanshen* in his book of the same name. 'Every revolution creates new words; the Chinese Revolution created a whole new vocabulary. A most important word was *fanshen*. Literally, it means to turn the body, to turn over. To China's hundreds of millions of landless peasants it meant to stand up; to throw off the landlord yoke, to gain land, stock, implements and houses. But it meant much more than this; it meant to throw off superstition and study science, to abolish word-blindness and learn to read, to cease considering women as chattels and establish equality between the sexes. It meant to enter a new world.'

Indeed, for most of the peasant millions revolution was the only alternative to death by war, flood, or famine, or a life made almost unbearable by landlord or state exactions. Police, education and judicial systems were based on the landlord class, and the tax-collectors were the agents of landlord officials. The rate of interest on loans was usually about thirty-five per cent, but reached as much as seventy-five per cent in some provinces in hard times. Edmund Clubb lists some forty-four taxes payable in Kansu including, for example, taxes on kettles, stockings, pigs, kindling wood and over-coats. Jan Myrdal translates these generalisations into terms of human suffering when he describes, for example, the hard life of a young boy sold by his parents to the landlord in lieu of the repayment of their debts. Another of Myrdal's villagers describes land reform as it went on in thousands of villages in the 1930s (and even more thoroughly in the late 1940s). 'The Land Department and the Poor Peasants Association decided to find out who were exploiters and who weren't . . . We were to take away the exploiters' posses-sions and give the exploited their land. We were very strict and energetic and destroyed the landowners as a class.'[10]

Gradually the message spread among the 'common people' that the Peasant and Workers' army was different from the war-lords' armies; that the Communist Party was different—it kept its promises of honest government and 'land to the tiller'. By November 1931 the Party was strong enough to summon its first general assembly in the town of Juichin, Kiangsi Province, where the creation of the Chinese Socialist Republic was announced. There were now two Chinas. At this time the Communists administered more than 3 000 counties with a population of some 50 million and an army of 300 000.

Chiang's Nationalist armies launched four bandit extermination campaigns; all failed, thanks to the Red's guerrilla tactics. 'When the enemy advances, we retreat; when he retreats we advance; when he stops we harass him; when he is tired we attack.' For his fifth campaign Chiang enlisted the help of the German general, von Seeckt, and this time he was successful.

The young Chinese Soviet was threatened: in July 1934 a proclamation was issued—but not of a retreat. 'The Chinese Red Army of Workers and Peasants will march north to resist the Japanese.'

The near legendary Long March had begun.

Ahead lay 368 days of traversing 7 000 miles of some of the most rugged and forbidding terrain in China, of struggle against bitter cold, bitter enemies, hunger and exhaustion. Tibor Mende comments that 'the Long March completed the Communists' already unrivalled knowledge of the Chinese peasants' psychology. It brought them into contact with new regions and different peoples, among whom they disseminated their ideas. They also learned a great deal about the problems and attitudes of the masses whom they were destined to govern later on.'[11]

The Red Army of Peasant and Workers was truly an apt description, for not only were virtually all the soldiers from these classes but their very existence depended on the food, shelter, scouts, interpreters, nurses, transport, and also the most important moral support of the common folk along the way. And even with such help life was precarious, as any collection of personal anecdotes of survivors simply and vividly records. An account of a typical incident with a minority people in Sikang in the far west is told in *Stories of the Long March*. The Tibetan villagers had all fled and red scouts went out to assure them their village was untouched and their lives safe. 'One by one they returned from the mountains driving some 37 000 sheep and cattle laden with bags of barley. With the headman in the lead they opened their doors and, despite our protestations, took us into their homes with great ceremony. Some unearthed bacon which had been buried underground and presented it to us. They also made a gift of three hundred animals to us. The women were mobilised to cook and boil water for a hundred sick and wounded fighters in the vicinity.'

'The Communists are like the seeds and the people are like the soil —the people are the sea and we are the fish who swim in it,' said Mao.

Journey's end was the now sacred place of the revolution, the ancient city of Yenan, in arid Shensi province, Northern China. Edgar Snow, the American journalist, was one of the few Westerners to hear the story of the march from the lips of its leaders soon after they had settled in Yenan, and he recorded this in his classic, *Red Star Over China*. 'Adventure, exploration, discovery, human courage and cowardice . . . suffering, sacrifice, loyalty, and then through it all, like a flame, this . . . amazing revolutionary optimism of those thousands of youths who would not admit defeat either by man or nature or God or death—all this and more are embodied in the history of an odyssey unequalled in modern times.'

In Yenan, through the years, Mao and his supporters consolidated their power, laid plans for the future and gradually attracted to their 'liberated areas' not only hundreds of thousands from the peasant classes, but also members of other classes in Chinese society, notably the intellectuals, from which, of course, some of the Party's most famous leaders had already been drawn. In the caves of Yenan Mao Tse-tung was to unite, for the first time in Chinese history, the two centuries-old forces of revolt: the common people, *Nung*, and the intellectuals.

中华民族是一个伟大的、富有革命传统的民族，百年以来热烈的爱国主义者进行着不屈不挠、再接再厉的英勇斗争。图为
一八四一年五月广州市郊、三元里人民自行发动反抗英国侵略者的斗争。

asant uprising. 'Shun was placed in charge of
ic affairs and they were well-administered and
eople were at peace; that indicated his accep-
e by the people. Heaven thus gave him the
ire; the people gave him the Empire. . . . In
Great Declaration it is said, "Heaven sees as
eople see; Heaven hears as my people hear".
vho outrages humanity is a scoundrel; he who
ges righteousness is a scourge . . . a despised
ure and no longer a king.' (Mencius, 300 BC)

They roared like thunder before San Yuan Li,
  A thousand, ten thousand, assembled all at once,
The villagers' force broke the enemy's ranks.
  Wives of one mind with their heroic men;
Mattocks and hoes turned weapons to hand.
  One brigade and then a hundred over the hills
beyond.
While barbarians looked on and suddenly paled.
(*A Collection of Opium War Literature* by A. Ying)

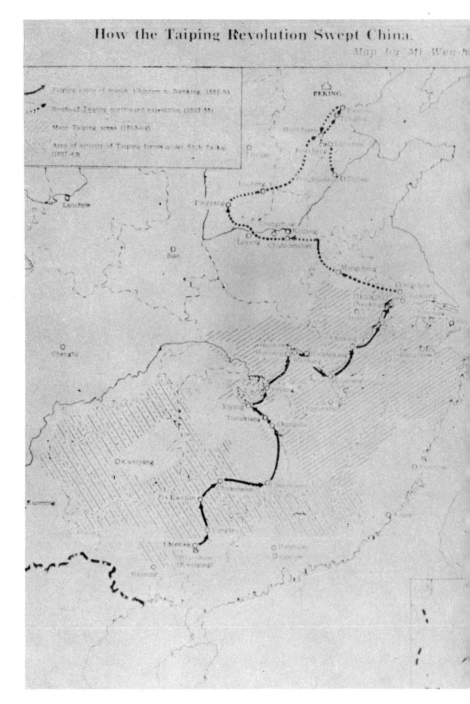

Map showing how the Taiping Rebellion sv
China.

Interior of a Taiping house. 'Where there is land let us till it together; where there is rice let us eat it together; where there is clothing let us wear it together; where there is money let us spend it together. . . . No place without equality, no-one cold or hungry.' (Taiping Creed)

A Boxer soldier. 'The *I Ho Tuan* [Boxer] Movement demonstrated once again that the peasant masses are the main force not only in the fight against feudalism but against imperialism also.'

Boxer show for recruiting. 'Attention: all people in markets and villages of all provinces in China—now, owing to the fact that Catholics and Protestants have vilified our gods and sages, have deceived our emperors and ministers above, and oppressed the Chinese people below, both our gods and our people are angry at them, yet we have to keep silent. This forces us to practise the *I-Ho* magic boxing so as to protect our country, expel the foreign bandits and kill Christian converts, in order to save our people from miserable suffering.

'After this notice is issued to instruct you villagers, no matter which village you are living in, if there are Christian converts, you ought to get rid of them quickly. The churches which belong to them should be unreservedly burned down.' (*China's Response to the West*, by Ssu-yu Feng and J. K. Fairbank)

Anti-Christian poster published by the Box depicting one of the stages of the Buddhist h

ng Ching-ling, Sun Yat-sen's wife. 'Sun was
king and speaking in terms of a revolution
would change the status of the Chinese
sant. Everything he planned he saw as a means
he betterment of the life of the Chinese peasant.
I remember clearly the first All-Kwangtung
sants' Conference in Canton in July 1924. For
first time we saw the people of China who must
her strength coming to participate in the
olution. From all the districts of Kwangtung
e the peasants, many of them walking miles and
es barefooted. They were ragged, tattered, some
ried baskets and poles. I was deeply moved.
Yat-sen was also. He said to me, "This is the
nning of the success of the revolution".' (*The
ggle for the New China*, by Soong Ching-ling)

A group of figures from the Rent Collection Court-yard in which are displayed sculptures of oppression. 'The poor have no land left. All the year round they work themselves to death without a day's rest, and when they have paid all their debts they live in constant anxiety they will be able to make both ends meet. The large landowners however live on the rents from their land, and are trouble free and carefree. Wealth and poverty are clearly separated.' (Lu Chih, c. AD 800)

A boy-slave. 'I was indentured to Sheng [landlord] to pay off my father's debt of $4. I was only fourteen. I was too small to carry buckets but all the same I had to carry water from the well so I half filled them and brought them that way.

'All the years I worked for Sheng, I never had a full stomach. I was hungry all the time and I was always cold as I never had clothes enough to keep warm. No matter how hard I worked I couldn't begin to pay off the debt. By the time I had been there seven years I owed him $15 not $4. At the end of each year he subtracted all the things I broke; the time I was sick and such things. He kept everything. I got no wage at all.' (*Report from a Chinese Village*, by Jan Myrdal)

遠高突惠圖
遠南頻年水旱民不
聊生辰轉溝壑道瑾
相望說傷連續人甲
聞另人係苦哉雨
種不得下托日托
長秋青葉換猪
及青黄集積
甫延枝根樹皮
智延命我国肥
其餘肢視視住
張脈脈京堂生
勒脈脈以
大黃防雷蔓臺最務
園民此電蘂臺義粉
世夜政果滿妻劉
視同奏
越耳

'There was extensive migration of the people from the dry regions, in some localities whole villages moving out. The sale of women and children, particularly young girls, reached such proportions that a special committee was organised for the protection of children. Prices ranged from $3.00 to $150.00, Chinese currency (one dollar in United States currency equals approximately two Chinese dollars), and thus the sacrifice of one or two of the younger members of the family served to provide the wherewithal to purchase food for the rest. Parents were not ready to give up their children but did so rather than see them starve.' (*China, Land of Famine*, by W. H. Mallory)

rving peasants were reduced to eating the bark n trees. 'The rise of the present peasant vement is a colossal event. In a very short time China's central, southern and northern pro-ces several hundred million peasants will rise a tornado or tempest, a force so extraordinarily ft and violent that no power, however great, be able to suppress it. They will break through the trammels that now bind them and dash ward along the road to liberation. They will d all imperialists, war-lords, corrupt officials, l bullies and bad gentry to their graves.' port on the Peasant Movement in Hunan, by Mao -tung)

An old peasant now living on a commu

Starving children at Chungkiang in 1

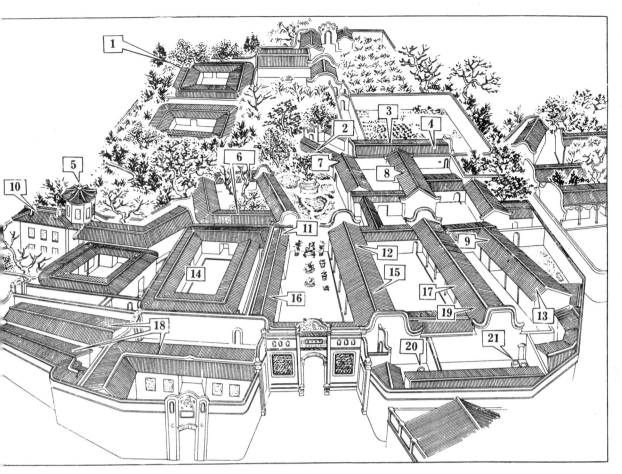

1   *Rent Collection Courtyard*
2   *Summer opium-smoking room*
3   *Granaries*
4   *Water dungeon*
5   *Tower of Joy*
6   *Storage-rooms*
7   *Hall of Pleasure*
8   *Buddhist prayer room*
9   *Third opium-smoking room*
10   *Boudoir*
11   *Counting house*
12   *Sitting-room (Chinese style)*
13   *Guest rooms for ladies*
14   *Servants' quarters*
15   *Sitting-room (Western style)*
16   *Reception room for sworn brothers*
    of secret societies
17   *Liu Wen-tsai's bed-room*
18   *Granaries*
19   *Second opium-smoking room*
20   *Servants' well*
21   *Master's well*

The manor house of a despotic landlord, Liu Wen-tsai. It is now a museum. Some landlords owned as many as twenty villages.

he proportion of vagabond elements is large and
ere are great masses of vagabonds in China.
me want to expand the army by recruiting almost
yone. But we must intensify education to counter
e vagabond outlook, draw active workers into
e ranks of the army. . . . We must not have a
ving bandit army.' (Mao Tse-tung, 1925)

Flailing: one of the agricultural tasks which the army undertook. 'The army must become one with the people so that they see it as their own army. Such an army will be invincible.' (Mao Tse-tung, 1938)

'Our army must be ruthless to our enemies . . . We must be kind to our own, to the people, to our comrades and subordinates and unite with them.' (1944)

Dr Norman Bethune, the Canadian doctor, operating on a patient in the guerrilla bases behind the Japanese lines in 1939. He is now a national hero in China.

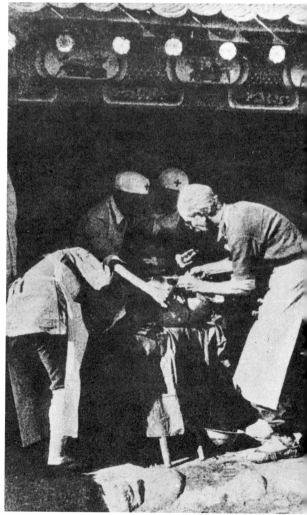

The literacy drive was continued after victory. A poster in the suburbs of Peking says: 'Socialism is paradise, but it will be hard for illiterates to enter there.'

A Chinese painting of the Red Army arriving in a village to recruit troops and give help with land reform. The Chinese Communist Party carried out the policies of 'a reasonable burden' and 'reduction of rent and interest', which weakened the feudal system of exploitation and improved the people's livelihood. This heightened the peasants' enthusiasm for the war of resistance and united the various anti-Japanese strata.

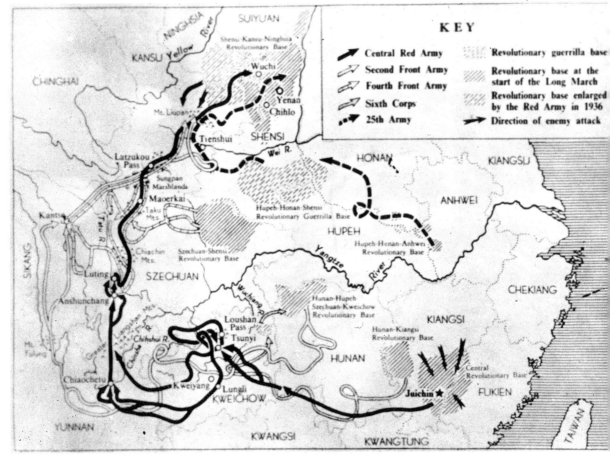

The routes of the Long March.

Crossing the grasslands on the Long March. '
prodigious feat of endurance . . . led across el
provinces, over remote regions inhabited
suspicious peoples . . . through murderous ma
lands overgrown by grass, and in the fac
danger from local and government forces.
claimed that the Communists crossed eigh
mountain chains, twenty-four large rivers, b
through armies of ten war-lords and defeated do
of KMT regiments; they took, temporarily, s
two cities. The basic aim—to save the revoluti
was achieved. But the price was high. Of
130 000 men who left fewer than 30 000 arriv
North Shensi [to join the guerrillas already i
region].' (*The Chinese Revolution*, by Tibor Me

e troops were continually on the march.
pite the lack of food and bad health they kept
marching. Little Hu . . . having gone without
for two days was desperately weak with
ger. His shoes were worn out and his legs
len. . . . When we entered the marshlands . . .
t men drank the bitter black water . . . and
grass and vegetables were now plucked and
n. When no green things were to be found the
would gather dried grass and chew the
s. . . . One day someone dug out a kind of
eous plant the size of a green turnip; it tasted
et and everybody at once searched for it. It
ved poisonous. Those who ate it vomited after
an hour and several died on the spot. Death,
ever, could not be allowed to delay our
gress.' (*Stories of the Long March*, F.L.P.)

Grinding barley on the Long March—a temporary drawing.

Liuting Bri

sants bringing fuel to the army.

the first time they came into contact with the
nal minority peoples of the South-western and
ern regions. . . . Finally, with their moral
re grown but physically and numerically
ened, the Communists began to organise
new base in Yenan.' (*The Chinese Revolution*,
ibor Mende)

The three leaders—Mao (centre), Chou (left)
Lin Paio—who were on the Long March toge

Journey's end: Ye

The whole policy of Communism and the arts was discussed during the Cultural Revolution by thousands of study groups poring over the booklet of the 1942 *Yenan Forum on Literature and the Arts* which had been republished and widely circulated. Parts of it were included in the little red book of quotations, set to music or recited in classrooms. Its influence is considerable. Its themes were touched on again in 1957; *Correct Handling of Contradictions Among the People*. Basically the message is that the arts must 'serve the people' and wage the class struggle.

Paintings and poems are to deal with deeds of revolutionary derring-do, with peasant labour-heroes or factory model workers. In the early 1950s there was a strong influence from the Soviet realist school with larger than life, romanticised presentations of such people. But at the same time several fine painters in the main classical tradition were honoured, and their paintings reproduced and widely sold, especially overseas. The best-known was Chi Pai-shih who died at the age of ninety-six, widely-mourned. During the ardours of the Cultural Revolution his work and that of Shu Pei-hung—almost equally famous for his magnificent 'black horse' ink paintings—was rarely seen. All was revolutionary exhortation, worker–peasant achievements. But the Forum has other points to make. 'A splendid culture was created during the long period of feudal society. To study the development of this old culture, to reject its feudal dross and assimilate its democratic essence is a necessary condition for developing our new national culture and increasing our national self confidence.'

So in 1971, when the Cultural Revolution was drawing to its close, it was not wholly surprising to open a copy of *China Pictorial* and find a double-page reproduction of something far more Chinese, far more traditional than had been seen in it for years. Its title? *The Spring Wind Blows Among Ten Thousand Willow Branches*. The theme of the painting is essentially modern and 'of the people', but there are also the traditional mountains and skyscapes, trees and winding streams; the human beings moving among them are, as in traditional paintings, inconspicuous, dwarfed by Nature; but they are active, engaged in harvesting or leading animals, carrying bright red flags. Among the trees, delicately etched against the sky, is a tall electricity pylon and on the fast-flowing river are a hydro-electric station and boats laden with commune-produce.

Soon after this the Foreign Language Press publications contained long accounts and excellent pictures of the numerous archaeological treasures which were quietly dug up during the storm and stress of the late 1960s. Though these archaeological finds were the property of the feudal landlords, they were the handiwork of the common people and are therefore to be valued as the products of skilled workers. An article accompanying photographs of these art treasures argued that such archaeological activities are far from reactionary, and that 'ancient cultural objects unearthed today are valuable material in our study of the politics, economics and culture of primitive slave and feudal societies'.[1]

In spite of exhortations to create a new Socialist art, the Party clearly is concerned to cherish its artistic heritage. Country folk are encouraged to become interested in and carefully look out for historical and cultural remains in their district.

Mao himself is a poet who writes in classical style for modern readers; he has little use for shoddy artistic standards. 'Works of art which lack artistic quality have no force, however progressive they are politically. Therefore we oppose both works of art with a wrong political viewpoint and the tendency to a poster and slogan style, which is correct in political viewpoint but lacking in artistic power.' No élite, no cognoscenti, are to inflict their taste upon the masses, but the masses in turn must learn to see when a work has no artistic power. 'First popularise', says Mao 'then refine.'

To popularise all must be encouraged to practise the arts as well as to view them. All communes and factories have poetry competitions and amateur drama and dance groups, and amateur art festivals are held frequently in the cities and country towns. Collective painting and sulpture are encouraged and great publicity was given to the Rent Collection Courtyard sculptures of life-sized clay figures representing scenes from the lives of tenants of a notorious Szechuan landlord. 'The work was created collectively by eighteen amateur and professional sculptors of Szechuan Province and put on permanent display in 1965 in the former manor house of Liu Wen-tsai, despot and big landlord. The work possesses a hard and clear political content.' It was shown also in the Imperial Palace Museum in Peking.

Theatrical productions are similarly to be group efforts not only by actors, designers, producers, but by the workers who paint and shift scenery, and stitch the costumes. Performers are not named in the programmes and 'stars' as such are discouraged.

It was in the theatre that the first big battle for establishing Mao's theory of the arts took place.

It started with the Festival of Peking Operas on contemporary themes in 1964. Peng Chen, then the powerful Mayor of Peking, commented on its success in 'maintaining socialist realism and serving the people'. In 1965 a senior Party member told cultural workers in Canton that they would no longer be producing, designing or acting in classical opera and they must see to it that this policy was quickly adopted: '. . . a little bit of coercion will do good; it will perhaps push things on a bit faster'. At the heart of the battle was Mao's wife, Chiang Ching, a former actress. She faced, at first, considerable opposition in her struggle for Peking opera with revolutionary themes. 'The socialist remoulding of some people in the opera schools and theatrical teams is still incomplete,' she complained.

But Mao's theory and Chiang Ching's practice were finally triumphant; a truly revolutionary repertory of opera was achieved and, side by side, revolutionary ballets choreographed and danced in Western style, but adapted to contemporary Chinese themes and moods. These ballets illustrate another facet of the Maoist approach to the arts. Just as artists must not reject all the past 'but weed through the old and let the new emerge', neither must they reject foreign styles and techniques—but 'they must make foreign things serve China' and not follow them slavishly; the ballet, therefore, displays many characteristics of its Russian origin, and the orchestras use many Western instruments and harmonies. Both ballets and operas are superbly staged and brilliantly performed. One opera, *Taking Tiger Mountain by Strategy*, celebrates the victory of its PLA hero over bandits, tigers and anti-peasant Nationalists; another, *Red Signal Lantern*, has for heroes and heroines railway workers and their families fighting against the Japanese as aids to the guerrillas, while the ballet *Red Detachment of Women* (which was staged for President Nixon) tells the story of women soldiers who fought with the Red Army on Hainan Island.

All are based on actual incidents and the companies went off before production started to the locales of the story where they talked with some of the people who had taken part in events described in the plays.

In a conversation with an Australian teaching in Peking, an old scholar commented: 'I was brought up to love the traditional opera but I do not miss it now, and my children have no use for those old dramas. What relation do they have to the lives and interests of Chinese youth today?'

Here is a winning entry from a commune poetry competition. Following the Yenan Forum line does not, it seems, preclude a sense of fun.

> On either end of a springy carrying pole,
> The girl balances two full buckets.
> Lithely she moves ahead not splashing a drop
> While the lad follows close behind.
> 'Stop for a moment', he begs her,
> 'Let me tell you the longing in my heart',
> Without pausing the girl laughs—
> 'Look at the beads of sweat on your face!
> You can't even keep pace
> With a woman carrying two full buckets!
> What has your heart got to say about that?'

Traditional theatre.

Actor making up for traditional theatre.

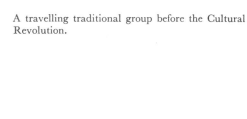
A travelling traditional group before the Cultural Revolution.

modern Peking opera, *Taking the Bandits'*
ghold.
e Six.
g enters:
hough I have come alone to the tiger's den,
illions of class brothers are by my side;
et vulture spew flames ten thousand leagues
gh, For the people I will fearlessly take this
monster on.

(Vulture (the bandit chief) takes his gun and shoots
out an oil lamp. Yang then takes a pistol from the
Bandit Chief of Staff and with one Shot knocks
out two oil lamps. The astonished bandits whisper
among themselves).
Culture to Yang:
What? You are . . .?
Yang:
I am a member of the Chinese People's Liberation
Army.
(Yang's army-mates rush into the bandits' den and
their victory in an exciting, highly acrobatic
free-for-all fracas, draws the opera to a close).

Boxwood carving.

The artist, Chi Pai-shih.

This painting, by Shu Pei-hung, is widely known in the West.

Modern ivory carvers have lost none of the skill of workers in the past.

Theatre troupe on tour in the mountains. 'Opera singers, poets and playrights should be sent stage by stage, group by group, to rural areas and factories. They must not stay all the time in the city . . . since useful things cannot be written in this way. . . . You will not be fed if you do not go to the lowest level.' (Mao Tse-tung, Spring Festival 1964)

Comrade Chiang Ching, first Deputy Leader of the Cultural Revolution Group under the Party Central Committee. 'There are well over 600 million workers, peasants and soldiers in our country whereas there is only a handful of landlords, rich peasants . . . rightists and *bourgeois* elements. Shall we serve this handful or the 600 million? We must stress operas on revolutionary themes which reflect real life in the fifteen years since the founding of the People's Republic and which create images of revolutionary heroes on our stage.' (*Revolution in Peking Opera*, F.L.P.)

the Peking Stadium there have been many
listhenics spectacles with the use of the 'human
saic' technique to present ever-changing pictures
a large-scale along the rising tiers of seats above
performers.

The great National Day procession along the
Changan Boulevard on 1 October every year
represents some half million marchers at least with
singers, dancers, acrobats, bands, militia, traditional
dragons and lions, and 'floats' on innumerable
aspects of the people's lives.

'All our literature and art are for the masses of the people . . . they are created for the workers, peasants and soldiers and are for their use. . . . Our literary and art workers must shift their stand and gradually move their feet over to the side of the proletariat.' (Mao Tse-tung, *Yenan Forum*)

Papercuts are a popular folk-art.

The ballet, *The White-haired Girl*. 'We must not reject the legacy of the . . . foreigners and refuse to learn from them [but they] should never take the place of our own creative work. . . . We must make foreign things serve China.' (Mao Tse-tung, *Yenan Forum*)

'It is imperative to separate the fine old culture of the people with a more or less revolutionary character from all the decadence of the old feudal classes.' (Mao Tse-tung) Instruments of a sixty-piece orchestra from the Chuichow region in eastern Kwangtung.

领导我们事业的核心力量
Lǐngdǎo Wǒmen Shìyè de Héxīn Lìliàng
(The Force at the Core Leading Our Cause Forward)

The force at the core leading our cause forward is the Chinese Communist Party. The theoretical basis guiding our thinking is Marxism-Leninism.

Just as the Red Army set to music many of its rules and aspirations, so today every factory and commune, every PLA unit, school and college produces its own songs and dances. There are also the national popular songs, mostly based on folk music and all with rousing themes and tunes. Best-known of all, 'The East is Red', is based on a Shansi folk song; others are favourite quotations from the Little Red Book set to music and sung—*molto vivace*.

Set of pottery figurines of acrobats and music of Western Han dynasty (206 BC–AD 24) fo at Tsinan in Shantung Province in 1969. ' historical relics unearthed during the Cult Revolution are a penetrating exposure of extravagant and decadent life led by the fet ruling classes [and the] exploitation of the labou people. (*China Pictorial*)

A suit of 'jade clothes with gold threads' (bu clothes of emperors and high-ranking aristoc of the Han dynasty) which was discovered i Western Han tomb in Mancheng County, H Province.

V Intellectuals and Politics

Those who are born with the possession of knowledge are the highest class of men. Those who learn and so readily get possession of knowledge are the next.' (Confucius)

Intellectuals have become an important factor in every aspect of our national life . . . To mobilise them more effectively and make fuller use of their abilities in our gigantic task of building socialism has become essential.' (Chou En-lai)

14 Intellectuals and Politics

From the most ancient times, intellectual life and political activity in China, have been indissolubly linked. The educated man, the scholar, was always a potential official, and only from the intellectuals were the officials recruited. To-day this national characteristic is manifested in the attempt to involve not only an educated minority but the whole nation, the people, in the combined intellectual and political life of the Chinese state. The distinction between the scholars and the illiterate must be eliminated, the class ranking of learned and uneducated destroyed. This is to be achieved not by the degradation of the learned, but by raising the national educational level until all can participate with equal opportunities. The Thought of Mao Tsetung, the new orthodox interpretation of Marxist-Leninist doctrine, is the guideline; it provides the texts and sets up the standards. The essence of his thought is precisely the indivisibility of intellectual activity and political life. 'Politics in Command', the slogan used at an earlier period of the Communist régime, remains the real directive. This means that all criticism must be constructive, not motivated by opposition to the system. Independent views and individualist attitudes cannot be publicised and must not be aired. All writing should be aimed at serving the people, that is, at promoting the purposes and policies of the régime. The distinction is unreal to the Chinese leadership; what furthers the objectives of Mao Tsetung's Thought is desirable and to be encouraged; what does not conform to this standard is contrary to the interests of the people, for his Thought is the true interpretation of those interests.

It is also true, of course, that this guideline provides wide scope for applied scientific investigation, technical development and scientific theory. The results of these activities will clearly serve the people. The scope for enquiry and thinking on such matters as history, sociology and economics is not so broad. History is still seen through Marxist spectacles; the succession of primitive Communism, slavery, feudalism, and capitalism having to run its course before Socialism can be achieved remains a fixed doctrine, although it is one which fits the facts of Chinese history very awkwardly. Sociology is necessarily under a similar constriction, and clearly economics cannot propound the theories of capitalist economics, except to demonstrate their errors.

There is thus a new orthodoxy, just as for so many centuries there was an old orthodoxy, Confucianism. The Chinese people have a tradition of conformity to the doctrines adopted by the ruling group, whether these are Confucian scholars or Marxist-Leninist-Maoist Communists. The old teaching expected all educated men to be at the disposal of the emperor for his service, if they were fitted for it; the new doctrine expects that every Chinese must study the Thought of Mao and fit himself for the service of the people. They must therefore understand the political aims of the people's government and subscribe to these purposes. They must be educated to do this; dumb obedience to a higher doctrine beyond their understanding is neither wanted nor tolerated. It is assumed—rather surprisingly to Western minds—that this universal education and politicisation of the nation will in fact produce a giant concensus in support of the Thought of Mao and its implementation. It would seem that the view that increased education could reinforce dissent and in time generate a real opposition is not thought significant or realistic in China.

Struggles for authority, such as that which accompanied the Cultural Revolution, are contests for the leadership and direction of the Communist Party and government, not attempts to substitute some other form of government. Just as those who rebelled against an emperor sought to displace him and rule in his stead—believing themselves better perhaps, but still within the same system of thought and politics—so the 'revisionists' and other opponents of Mao Tse-tung are also Communists, but are charged with planning to direct the Communist system on lines contrary to or divergent from his ideas. In certain aspects China has not escaped from her past, in spite of social revolution and sweeping change.

Not only the Communists agreed that the Confucian orthodoxy, the pattern of the imperial past, was outworn, unadaptable, and ill-fitted to cope with the problems of the contemporary world. Framed when China was the only civilisation with which the Chinese people had contact, it had no competitors for many centuries. By the end of the nineteenth century the younger generation of Chinese associated the existing orthodoxy with decline, dynastic decay, national weakness and purblind conservatism. The alien Manchu dynasty was condemned on the double grounds of being alien and being antiquated. This revolutionary generation was inspired by Western ideas learned in study abroad in Europe and America. At first their new policies were strictly imitative of the West. China should be a republic (the most modern form of government), and should have a parliamentary régime under the rule of law. Nationalism, then seen as the right and duty of all citizens, must be expressed in the building of a strong, free nation, no longer cowed by foreigners.

The revolutionaries of 1912 were singularly preoccupied with these questions of political forms and quite unaware of the social problems which underlay the decay of the old régime. They had no coherent or precise plans for land reform, for the alleviation of peasant poverty, nor for fundamental economic reforms. They firmly believed in education, but saw the attainment of universal literacy as something far in the future and were more concerned with re-educating the urban and literate youth in the new ideals of democracy. Their belief in the virtues of the institutions based on Western models which they hoped to introduce to China was not grounded on any deep knowledge of the actual conditions of Chinese life and its social and economic problems. They were young, and they had spent most of their adult lives studying abroad. Thus, by hindsight, it is not surprising that the first revolution failed to do more than dethrone a decadent dynasty. It was followed by political confusion, but also by intellectual ferment. Politics and the intellectuals were now divorced; the political life of the nation was directed by groups of corrupt and reactionary militarists; the scholars, cut off from their old field of activity, flocked to staff the new universities, which became centres of the most active political and philosophic speculation.

The next generation, those who matured in this age of confusion, soon found that the doctrines brought from the West were inadequate. Democracy required an educated people, and also the operation of an established and respected system of law. This was wholly lacking, since the old Chinese polity did not recognise any but criminal law, had no legal profession, and had left civil law to the arbitration of concerned groups and organisations, merchant guilds, village elders, clan heads, and other bodies who had direct interest in the dispute. The concept of a 'loyal opposition' was totally alien to Chinese tradition and thinking; it could not be abruptly transplanted from societies with very different histories and formation. Law never became respected, enforced—or even to any real degree enacted. Democracy foundered in the militarist era which soon followed the revolution of 1912, but Nationalism remained, stimulated by the continuing spectacle of China's weakness and the aggressive or domineering attitude of the foreign powers, in particular Japan. Dr Sun's revolutionary Party was refounded as the Nationalist Party (Kuomintang) with a programme dedicated to the recovery of China's sovereign rights and lost territories, but it did not seriously attempt to put forward a policy of social or economic reform, and this lack was to prove its weakness and cause its failure. In 1921, under the inspiration and guidance of the Russian Revolution, the Chinese Communist Party was formed with eleven members, one of whom was Mao Tse-tung.

The introduction of Marxist ideas, a direct consequence of the Russian Revolution, had preceded the foundation of the Chinese Communist Party. Apart from a very few foreign-trained intellectuals, it is unlikely that there had been in China, any knowledge of the Communist doctrines prior to the Bolshevik revolution. But the impact of that event was very great, for in it the Chinese intellectuals saw the solution to their own country's plight. Russia also, had been a decadent empire and assailed by outside enemies. The Communist revolution seemed to give her new internal strength, cohesion and purpose, and to provide a defence against external pressure and interference which was soon respected. Marxism became fashionable in Chinese educated circles; the novelists took the tone, the students studied the new doctrine, and many of their professors became converted. It was from the intellectual ferment of the universities, above all Peking National University, that the Chinese Communist movement was born, and it was staff members of that university who formed and led the infant Chinese Communist Party.

Outside observers of China have often doubted whether the Chinese people could have an inclination to Communism; it has been argued that they are an individualistic people, keen merchants and successful capitalists. These considerations, however, do not apply fully to all classes. The peasants had an old tradition of co-operation which could be, and has been used as, the foundation for new forms of collective organisation. The scholars had the solidarity of their élite class, the governing class of two millennia, but were now dispossessed. Determined to recover status, and also disillusioned with the orthodoxy to which their forefathers had so long clung, they wanted a new doctrine, one which would be modern and would not open the gate to further foreign domination. It should not be a close copy of a Western system, since these had failed. In many respects Marxism filled the bill. It was the most up-to-date Western political theory; it was not the one which the Western imperialist nations accepted, and it was one which would oppose their pretensions. Above all it was comprehensive, authoritarian, a true alternative to the discarded imperial Confucian orthodoxy. It was, moreover, a doctrine which the imperialist Western nations violently opposed, rejected and disowned. Therefore it must have something for China, since that which my enemy dislikes is probably desirable for me. It seems certain that these ideological and psychological impulses first inclined the Chinese intellectuals towards Communism, not the social and economic doctrines. The latter were neither widely understood nor considered with great attention.

Only a minority had fully accepted the Communist doctrine although left wing ideas were prevalent in the early 1920s. The climate was opposed to all reaction and increasingly hostile to the liberal views associated with Western democratic forms of government. Nationalism was a very strong common motive among all educated men and was soon to spread deeper into the whole population. The Chinese people and its intellectual leaders were still groping for the system and the solution which would fit their tradition and their temperament. It has been the experience of the Chinese people throughout their history that a major foreign innovation, particularly an intellectual concept, has had to undergo profound transformation and modification before it becomes truly acceptable and viable in China. Buddhism was introduced in the third century AD but it was not fully integrated into the Chinese civilisation until at least the fifth century AD by which time it was much changed from the form and practices that had prevailed in the mother country, India. Western ideas, imported into China in the nineteenth century, have undergone and are still undergoing a similar transformation. Those ideas and systems which proved too alien to the Chinese have been discarded and almost forgotten; those which were useful for a time, more as conveyors of foreign learning than by virtue of their own appeal (and Christianity fell into this class), flourished to a certain degree, but have now lost support and are dwindling rapidly. The Chinese people needed a foreign doctrine to fertilise their own culture which had become stagnant; in Communism they found one which they could reshape in their own way, which was modern, but not associated with the countries which had been regarded as the enemies of China. When, in due course, Russia, the source of Communism, showed herself inclined to assume the attitudes and ambitions of a great power, the Chinese repudiated the Russian connection and further modified their Communist doctrines to suit Chinese ideas and practice.

One of the main obstacles to the rapid modernisation of China, in comparison with the modern history of Japan, is precisely that the Chinese culture is creative, and not adaptive. The Chinese language does not easily accept foreign words; they have to be translated to become current; the Chinese people need to feel that some new custom or institution has become Chinese before they respect it. The urge to change anything foreign into something more recognisably Chinese is strong, probably unconscious, but obvious to the observer. It was a hindrance to the adoption and operation of foreign institutions and the acceptance of foreign ideology. It long seemed clear that whatever the Chinese reaction to other Western innovations might be, they had whole-heartedly accepted the superior achievements of Western medical science. But in recent years the revival and scientific study and application of the ancient Chinese medical practice of acupuncture has once again demonstrated the innate drive to make every branch of learning more Chinese, to integrate every aspect of modern civilisation with the Chinese cultural tradition. To the

Chinese the foreign idea and invention becomes a stimulant, rather than remains a model. The stimulant drives them to change, modify and above all to integrate the new into the old, even if, as is now the case, the tradition itself is undergoing change, selection and reinterpretation.

The history of the Chinese intellectuals in the twentieth century was made in an environment where these conflicting forces were actively engaged. There was at once acceptance, emulation of the West, and rejection of the consequences of such a relationship. Nationalism in its modern form was derived from Western models; the Chinese had strong racial or ethnic consciousness and sense of identity, but in imperial times there was no reason to evoke the political nationalism of modern times. For centuries it lacked the stimulus of powerful rival nations of equal cultural level, and it was not until the pressures of the Western foreign countries aroused the Chinese intellectuals that Chinese nationalism was born. It was then directed as much against the alien Manchu dynasty, as against the foreigner from beyond the sea. But, as it was increasingly directed against the imperialist powers, including Japan, it became the dominant intellectual and political movement in the 1920s. Since the Manchus, now dethroned, counted for nothing, it ceased to be anti-Manchu, and became obsessed with the encroachment of the foreign powers. The movement was relatively unconcerned with the condition of the Chinese people, although many observers could point out that China's weakness in the face of the foreigner was a corollary to her internal weakness and social disorder.

The Communist Party, at first tightly led by disciples of the Comintern, was urban in personnel and in operation. It directed its attention to the economic plight of the workers, but paid less heed to that of the peasants. Following Russian precepts it sought to promote strikes, rouse the proletariat of the cities, and hinder the operations of the capitalists and the foreign firms established in Chinese Treaty Ports. Indeed, this is one reason why the overthrow of capitalism evoked much less emotion and regret in China than similar events in other countries which have experienced a Communist revolution. As far as the masses were concerned Capitalism was a form of foreign imperialism which existed among the Chinese only on a relatively small scale. Such large Chinese firms as did exist were seen as subsidiaries or partners of the foreigner. In effect they often were. Equally, in the early 1920s, there was no real Chinese proletariat on any considerable scale. Shanghai had its industrial workers, very ill paid, and easily replaced if they resisted their treatment. There were pockets of potential proletarian support in some provincial centres of railway enterprise and mining, but these were scattered, and isolated. The lowly paid artisans and coolies of the inland cities were not a proletariat, but a class so depressed that they lived from day to day with no time for thought of the morrow.

The Communist Party, therefore, appealed to young intellectuals and to a small number of industrial workers; as yet it neither touched the peasants nor stirred the majority of the nation. It was seen as a left-wing subsidiary of the Kuomintang or Nationalist Party. Not until the great anti-foreign agitation of 1925, following the shooting of student demonstrators by the Settlement police in Shanghai, did the Communist Party begin to make real headway, and then it was only in coalition with the Nationalists, and still under the often mistaken direction of officers sent to China by the Comintern. To become 'Chinese', the Communist Party had to shed this leadership and find a way of penetrating the mass of the people, not merely the modernised intellectuals and the industrial workers of a very few cities. At this time, and for long after, the main stream of the Chinese intellectuals were ardent nationalists, rather left-wing but vague in their social thinking, rejecting the West to an increasing degree but accepting the modern learning from the West, and as yet only to a small extent convinced that Marxism was the solution to China's problems.

The transformation from this attitude to growing support for the Communist doctrine and Party was brought about by the war with Japan. During that struggle the weakness and corruption of the Nationalist régime was very clearly revealed, more clearly in Chungking than it had been in Nanking. Intellectuals turned against it, and national-minded, patriotic Chinese were disgusted by the inertia and apathy and also by the pursuit of power politics against the national interest. The Communists were fighting the enemy; the fact could not be hidden even by a controlled press, since many lines of contact with the occupied areas remained open. Sympathy for their activity overcame reluctance about their programme; the middle view, that whatever the outcome of the war no further civil war was acceptable, was the dominant view. Coalition, compromise, but no civil war. This hope was destroyed, mainly, as General Marshall made clear in his report to President Truman, by the unwillingness of Chiang Kai-shek to make any significant concession and his barely concealed hope thot he could crush the Communists with his American-armed forces.

When the civil war came, the movement of opinion swung swiftly towards the Communist side because of the inefficiency, corruption and low morale of the Nationalist government and forces. It was soon seen that a Communist victory was inevitable. The middle class had been ruined by inflation; they no longer feared the loss of property and wealth, for they had little left. Everyone wanted peace, and peace by Communist victory seemed the best and quickest hope. By the end of 1948 the régime of Chiang Kai-shek had lost all popular and intellectual support and was morally bankrupt.

15 The Intellectual and the People's Republic

'Intellectuals' is still a word of special meaning to the Chinese since the scholar has been, for centuries, the peak of the social pyramid. The intellectual class—literally the 'learned elements'—included anyone who had graduated from Senior Middle (high) school. From the inception of the People's Republic the Communists have sought to harness the prestige and the skills of this class and to multiply it many times by giving educational facilities the highest priority even at a time when the devastated country was crying out for factories, housing and communications. There were to be schools, universities, teachers' and technical colleges, but they were to produce a new kind of intellectual educated to 'serve the people', to know that 'professional knowledge must be combined with politics'—indeed, that 'education is politics'.[1]

Academic work began to reach international standards as Western scholars, who were visiting China in increasing numbers by the early 1960s, reported. 'Chinese scientists seem fantastically well-acquainted with Western scientific literature. There is a lot of good work being done that anyone in Europe would be glad to have in his own laboratory,' commented Sir Lindon Brown, Vice-President of the British Royal Society, in 1962. But for Mao and his supporters there were still many doubts about students' and teachers' revolutionary dedication. In October 1951 Chairman Mao Tse-tung declared: 'The remoulding of ideology . . . of the various types of intellectuals is an important condition for the thorough carrying out of democratic reforms in various fields.'

Shortly after, in the 'self-education campaign' of 1952, teachers, through a series of discussions, were asked to re-evaluate their attitudes and ideas and methods in the light of the needs of their country. 'The university teachers have learned by their own experience that the method of criticism and self-criticism is the best way of improving one's work.'[2]

It was the very strength of the intellectual tradition that made it a two-edged sword; dedicated to the dictatorship of the proletariat, the Party feared 'ivory towerism', scholarly detachment from the class struggle, from the workers, peasants and soldiers. It also feared, though far less, active counter-revolutionary moves. So the intellectuals' role received a great deal of attention, for their attitude could affect immeasurably the history of the present as it had that of the past. The Party agreed with Mao. 'Ideological reform of the intellectuals is one of the most important conditions for our country's all out democratic reform and gradual industrialisation . . . The intellectuals will accomplish nothing if they fail to integrate themselves with the workers and peasants. In the final analysis, the dividing line between revolutionary intellectuals and non-revolutionary or counter-revolutionary intellectuals is whether or not they are willing to integrate themselves with the workers and peasants and actually do so.'

In one of his most famous treatises, *On the Correct Handling of Contradictions Among the People*, published in 1957, Mao devoted much attention to the development of the intellectuals in the previous decade and stated that it would 'take a fairly long time to decide the issue in the ideological struggle between capitalism and socialism' because the influence of the *bourgeois* intellectuals would continue. But, on the whole, Mao seems to be reasonably confident that their role will be beneficial and their conversion reasonably easy, given time.

'The vast majority of students trained in the old schools and colleges can integrate themselves with the workers, peasants and soldiers; they must be re-educated by them under the guidance of the correct line and thoroughly change their political ideology. Such intellectuals will be welcomed by the workers, peasants and soldiers.'

The Chinese Communists, from the start, have been nothing if not pragmatic and were very well aware that reconstruction of the shattered economy was impossible without trained minds for administration and teaching, for launching huge industrial programmes and housing projects; they were also aware that the workers might not be wholly helpful in this. 'We should trust the intellectuals who are willing to serve the cause of socialism . . . Many of our comrades are not good at getting along with the intellectuals. They are stiff with them, lack respect for their work and interfere in scientific and cultural work in a way that is not called for,' said Mao.

There was a further problem in the early days of the republic. Almost all the senior intellectuals had received a Western-style education either in missionary institutions in China or on scholarships to American and European universities. 'The imperialist powers have never slackened their efforts to poison the minds of the Chinese people, that is, to carry out a policy of cultural aggression.'

Nevertheless, of the 100 000 highly-qualified scholars, ninety per cent stayed on to serve their country. Dr Wu Y Feng's brief account of her attitudes and experiences given to the writer in 1963 is typical of those of many of her fellows: 'My father was a Manchu official. I graduated from Shanghai University in the 1920s and took my PhD from Michigan. When I returned to China I became Principal of the Women's Christian College in the University of Nanking. I worked hard with Mde. Chiang Kai-shek's Women's Comfort Association in 1927 and in 1938 became one of the ten women on the KMT People's Consultative Council. I disapproved of my students' interest in the CCP until I slowly realised that the whole country was slipping into chaos because of corruption and disorganisation. Desperate measures were needed. My students' interest in reform should not be checked. We've run the college for too long like a New England Girls' finishing school, I decided. Finally, I threw in my lot with the new government—still a Christian, of course.'

Dr Wu became Vice Minister of Education and, later, Vice-President of the province's National Assembly.

In the early 1950s the Party, with characteristic doctrinal and organisational vigour, immediately set about the elusive task of remoulding old-time intellectuals who had to join the mass study-movement of the time. Millions of hours were spent in criticism-self-criticism sessions, in detailed self-analysis, on writing reports of past errors of thought, past self-centredness and 'ivory towerism'. Quaker professor, William Sewell, gives one of the best accounts of what this involved for him and his Chinese colleagues in a Christian university when a senior Communist Party cadre arrived on the campus.

'How is your thought? Is it advancing? Are you succeeding in making it deeper? These were the questions that serious young men and women, and also their teachers, were asking each other when they met on the campus at Jen Dah. They no longer enquired about ... trivial things ... life was concerned with matters which were much more vital ... It was now our business to put our minds in order, to deepen our thoughts, to criticise each other and ourselves, so that we could be undivided and efficient in our work for the coming of true Socialism ... He talked of us as individuals, but always seen in connection with society, never as islands ... The way back was to examine our thoughts one by one, track down the source of those which were evil, see how they had grown within us, and then ruthlessly eradicate them.

'"Sit down as at a desk", he told us, "bring out your mind and lay it as a book before you. Then, objectively, not thinking of it as yourself, slowly and patiently turn over the pages one by one. There is much that you will have forgotten, much that will return only fragment by fragment, so you must read the book again and yet again. Share what you read with each other, for in sharing you will remember more.

'"In the book you arc looking at, you will find things that are evil. Bring each evil thing out from the page. Place them one by one on the table before you, examine each in detail; then when you have learnt all about them throw them away . . . take all the dirty things and wash them clean. Make yourselves into new men and new women for the New Democracy of China."

'He sped us to our groups with the final words, "You must work. You must act".'[3]

By 1955 there was apparently a need for a further rectification campaign against the intelligentsia, who were showing 'signs of reverting to feudal practices and concepts'. A literary critic and writer, Hu Feng,* was the storm-centre of what was referred to as 'the campaign against reactionary Hu Feng elements'. An extract from Chou En-lai's *Report on the Question of Intellectuals* in 1956 makes clear the unease. 'Certain irrational features in our treatment of intellectuals and certain sectarian attitudes by some of our comrades towards intellectuals outside the Party have handicapped us in bringing their strength into full play . . . We must ceaselessly raise their political consciousness and rely on their close . . . fraternal alliance of workers, peasants and intellectuals.'

In January 1956 Mao made a speech to a Supreme State Conference which was not published verbatim, but interpreted by Lu Ting-yi, Propaganda Minister. 'To writers we say, "Let a hundred flowers bloom"; to scientists we say, "Let a hundred schools of thought contend" . . . as the people's political power becomes progressively consolidated such freedom should be given even fuller scope.'

After a short period of doubt and hesitancy the floodgates were opened, and many schools of thought contended that the Party became apprehensive. Many intellectuals claimed to be wasted in menial positions, scientists and teachers to be dominated by bureaucratic party cadres; artists felt they had to conform, teachers objected

* According to Edgar Snow, Hu Feng had attacked Mao as 'an imbecile, a rotten beast'.

to long study hours on Marxist thought; the complaints flowed in. Edgar Snow commen'ed in *The Other Side of the River*: 'Tensions of this nature under Stalinism had always been resolved by secret arrests, mass purges . . . Mao took a new and subtle approach when he published in June 1967, *On the Correct Handling of Contradictions Among the People*, a document of first importance in the literature of contemporary Marxism.'

Mao makes his famous distinction between antagonistic contradictions such as those between the capitalist and Socialist systems, and non-antagonistic contradictions between people basically in agreement on political concepts. Indeed, said Mao, 'Contradictory forces are the very forces which move society forward [but] the essential thing is to start with a desire for unity'.

'It is not only necessary but possible for large numbers of our intellectuals to change their world outlook. But a thorough change . . . takes quite a long time, and we should go about it patiently and not be impetuous. Actually there are bound to be some who are reluctant to accept Marxism-Leninism and Communism. We should not be too exacting in what we expect of them . . . As long as they engage in legitimate pursuits we should give them opportunities for suitable work . . . They should study Marxism-Leninism, current events and political affairs. Both students and intellectuals must study hard . . . Not to have a correct political point of view is like having no soul . . . Let a hundred flowers blossom and let a hundred schools of thought contend. How did these slogans come to be put forward? They were put forward on the basis of the recognition that various kinds of contradictions still exist . . . Different classes . . . have their own views on what are fragrant flowers and what are poisonous weeds. What, from the point of view of the broad masses . . . should be the criteria for distinguishing between flowers and poisonous weeds?'

Mao answers his question by giving six criteria of which the most important are that words and actions must benefit socialist construction and the people's democratic dictatorship, and that they must tend to strengthen the leadership of the Party. He then adds, characteristically, 'Ideological remoulding in the past was necessary and yielded some good result . . . but it was carried on in a somewhat rough and ready way and the feelings of some people were hurt— this was not good. We must avoid such shortcomings in future.'

After some three years during which national attention was fixed mostly on the intellectuals it shifted in 1958 to the peasants and their communes, to the industrial workers and the Great Leap Forward: 'We Will Catch Up with Britain in 15 Years'. But the intelligentsia, though a little in the background, were as necessary as ever and their integration with rural and city workers was essential. Theorising and exhortation was not enough: 'Dogma is less use than cowdung,' declared Mao. Practice, action, must follow theorising.

On 4 May 1957 the Central Committee of the Communist Party of China issued a directive on the intellectuals' need to undertake manual labour. 'Not a few comrades who were influenced by the thinking of the exploiting classes of the old society have now forgotten this excellent tradition, and they look down on physical labor. A concern for fame, advantage, and position is growing among them . . . In principle all Communists irrespective of their position and seniority should assume similar and equal work as ordinary laborers . . . This is a great test for Communists: whether they can work for the Party's general task under the new historical constitution.'

And a great test for Communists it certainly proved to be. 'The question of cadres confronting the working class is an organisational task unprecedented in human history', said the Party journal, *Red Flag.* To be 'Red' or 'expert'—that was the question. Could the *bourgeois* and upper-class 'learned-elements' be both? Chen Yi, the Foreign Minister, speaking to graduates of Higher Institutes in Peking in 1961, thought they could. 'I want to say a few words about those youths who came from the exploiting classes. . . We should not emphasise their family origin. A youth cannot help whether he came from an exploiting family or a worker peasant family. Being born into the exploiting class does not hinder his becoming a revolutionary. I hope you [graduates] will go to the poorest areas . . . go wherever your fatherland needs you . . . to the most difficult places . . . Your ideological level is still not high enough.'

Of course by far the greatest upheaval in the lives of both old and new intellectuals came with the Great Proletarian Cultural Revolution—all three epithets are fully justified!

It was not until 1966 that the historic title was bestowed upon this upheaval, but as the torrents of debate gushed forth it became clear that there had been several years of interparty schisms on both doctrinal and practical aspects of the educational, cultural, scientific and social scene. It was an interparty struggle, not to any serious degree a counter-revolutionary one, perhaps its most extraordinary feature being that its directives came from the top; above all from Mao himself, demanding, at the risk of the disintegration of all he had striven for, a root and branch soul-searching and reconstruction of his Party. 'If there were no contradictions in the Party, no ideological struggles to resolve them, the Party's life would come to an end.'

Mao's *Talks at the Yenan Forum on Literature and the Arts*, given originally in 1942, was reissued in the mid 1960s and discussed by millions. One paragraph in that could serve as the text for the Cultural Revolution: 'Intellectuals who want to integrate themselves with the masses, who want to serve the masses, must go through a process in which they and the masses come to know each other well. . .' This concept was expanded in *Handling Contradictions* in 1957.

It is now generally accepted that the real opening of the Cultural Revolution was the dismissal of the Defence Minister, Peng Te-hui, at the Party conference in Lushan in 1959. The *Peking Review* of 18 August 1967 said: 'The struggle at Lushan is a class struggle, a continuation of the life and death struggle between the major antagonistic classes—the *bourgeoisie* and the proletariat—which has gone on all through the Socialist revolution in the last ten years. This kind of struggle, it seems, will continue in China and in our Party for at least twenty years and possibly half a century . . .' Next came attacks on well-known Party writers, including the prestigious Wu Han, Vice-Major of Peking; this was followed by Mao's own *Five Militant Documents on Literature and the Arts*, whose practitioners, he complained, 'have acted like high and mighty bureaucrats and not carried out the policies of the Party'. Practice must conform to theory, so in 1964, Peking witnessed a great 'Festival of Peking Operas on Revolutionary Themes', in the organisation of which Mao's wife, former actress Chiang Ching, emerged as the leading revolutionary lady.

'According to a rough estimate there are 3 000 theatrical companies in the country (not including amateur troupes). The professional operatic stage is occupied by emperors, princes . . . scholars and beauties, and on top of these, ghosts and monsters. The drama companies, too, lay stress on producing . . . foreign plays and plays on ancient themes. So we can say that the modern drama stage is also occupied by ancient Chinese and foreign figures . . . May I ask which class stand do artists take? And where is the artists' conscience which you talk about?'

The plot thickened throughout 1964 with a blistering attack on a play by Wu Han and the revelation by Marshall Lin Piao that the PLA was having its Cultural Revolution, too. Still no firm indication was given as to which of the highest Party members were under attack, though the famous circular of the Central Committee, May 1967, referred ominously to 'some still trusted by us . . . and nestling beside us.'

But the fat was really in the fire, with the appearance of the now historic 'big character poster' on the walls of Peking University, 'Sweep Away All Monsters', which 'sounded the first volley of guns in the great proletarian revolution'. It read, in part: 'The proletarian cultural revolution is aimed not only at demolishing the old ideology and culture and all the old customs and habits . . . but also at creating and fostering among the masses an entirely new ideology and culture and entirely new customs and habits—those of the proletariat'.

On Mao's request the whole poster was broadcast on Peking Radio. 'The single spark started prairie fires' and literally millions of big character posters appeared across the country. One by one, the leading 'revisionists', the *bourgeois* elements, were being unseated— or 'unhorsed', as a favourite word had it.

Mao himself produced a poster, 'Bombard the Headquarters', and the 8 August circular of the CCP's Central Committee presented the *Sixteen Points* on the Cultural Revolution's character and aims, many of them relevant in the context of this chapter.

Point 1, for example, declares that in the Cultural Revolution, which 'touches people to their very souls, the proletariat must use its new ideas and culture to counteract the lingering *bourgeois* cultural influences, against which young people especially must make revolution'.

Point 2 is more specific on the position of the intellectual: 'As regards scientists, technical assistants . . . as long as they are patriotic and are not against the Party and socialism we should continue to apply the policy of unity-criticism-unity . . . Special care should be taken of those scientists and scientific and technical personnel who have made contributions. Efforts should be made to transform their world outlook and style of work.'

Point 10 stresses the need to reform the education system so that those being educated can develop morally, intellectually and physically (with the help of 'productive labour') and become 'labourers with a Socialist consciousness and culture'.

Overseas, fears of cultural purges were widely voiced, and, in Peking, vigorously rebutted. 'China's great proletarian cultural revolution is directed against . . . a handful of anti-Party, anti-Socialist, counter-revolutionary *bourgeois* intellectuals. With regard to the greater number of intellectuals who came over from the old society, our policy is to unite with them, educate and remould them. And the ranks of proletarian intellectuals are steadily growing.'[4]

At last 'China's Kruschev, the top Party person in authority taking the capitalist road' was named. Liu Shao-chi is, like Mao, a Hunanese and was Mao's close colleague from the 1920s. He is accused of the arch-crime of 'revisionism', the watering-down or perversion of Marxism-Leninism, a reversion to capitalist social and economic concepts. Formerly Head of State, he is now 'a renegade, traitor and scab', under some form of house detention, a non-person in both Party and government.

And so to the Red Guards. Their movement started in the middle schools and universities, was blessed by Mao and spread throughout the country absorbing young workers and peasants and, later, older ones, too. They travelled free on the trains and buses; they undertook 'little Long Marches' to 'steel themselves', they 'learned to make revolution and study revolutionary history' making themselves 'the target of revolution' and always, always, learning how to serve the people by following the example of the masses and studying Mao's Thought, especially as embodied in the little red book of which tens of millions of copies were distributed. Every Red Guard carried one as his or her anti-revisionist weapon.

China Pictorial reported: 'The Red Guards appeared at their first mass rally in Peking, at five o'clock on 18 August 1966. When the sun had just risen above the eastern horizon Chairman Mao arrived at Tien Anmen Square which was covered by a vast sea of people and a forest of red flags . . . The square was seething with excitement. People raised their hands and jumped and cheered and clapped. Many shed tears of joy . . . Elated they exclaimed "Chairman Mao is here". The crescendo of cheers shook the sky over the capital.'

The next instruction was that 'The Red Guards and the revolutionary teachers should go to the countryside to take part in manual labour . . . and learn the diligence, revolutionary enthusiasm and other fine qualities of the working people. Take firm hold of revolution and stimulate production.' Off they went in their thousands.

China's Foreign Language Press publications were filled with accounts of intellectuals learning to 'make revolution' in the country, learning 'to become one with the masses.'

In 1971 a group of British visitors had a long interview with a Professor of Dynamics: 'He had worked in three different factories alongside the workers, at the same time giving them lectures in his subject. In this way the meaning of labor became real to him—and at the same time it was possible for the workers to comprehend the work of an intellectual and its practical application.'[5]

'It is right to rebel' was one of Mao's mottoes for the students and workers; and rebel they did by the hundred thousand. Greeted at first as welcome 'shock troops' the Red Guards later fell into faction fighting or lost interest. Hard work on farms and in factories, 'little Long Marches' and Party discipline discouraged and disillusioned some. In 1968 Chou En-lai, greatly admired by the young, spoke out, criticising the Red Guards who had been 'quite daring in the earlier stages of the rebellion; but, after alliances have been formed two-thirds of the members have left. Can this be called revolution? This is a manifestation of *petit bourgeois* vacillation. They think they should take a rest and take things easy after making revolution for a year or so. Some have gone back home; some have turned to love, played poker and degenerated. A few have pasted up reactionary slogans.'

Mao and Lin Piao specifically warned against violence, but some violence there was, and some killing: the PLA were needed to check it. In Wuhan serious struggles occurred.

Gradually, the Red Guard and all other youngsters were told to return to the schools and colleges which were reopening one by one. Clearly neither schools nor scholars could be the same again after they had heeded the main directive: 'Carry out the Cultural Revolution thoroughly and transform the education system completely'. To ensure that the intellectuals would become 'one with the masses', the whole education system was to be retooled. 'Learned elements' must become 'revolutionary intellectuals'. All China's Foreign Language Press publications have for years contained accounts by professors, teachers, technologists, journalists and writers telling how they worked with tea-pickers, pig-tenders, stokers, weavers and bricklayers, learning from them the lessons of revolution, the need for perpetual vigilance against 'taking the capitalist road' like Liu Shiao-chi. They tell how they learned, also, a good deal of practical know-how in their own subjects, for efforts were made to relate manual labour to academic work as far as possible. In turn, the academics taught the peasants the theory that explained their practice.

More and more exhortations and directives were issued demanding a change of heart, a change of direction from purely academic studies to that vital amalgam of mental and manual, of worker and intellectual. Big character posters on education appeared on thousands of school and college noticeboards; thousands of speeches were made condemning reactionary and revisionist economic and educational trends.

A much-discussed article appeared in *Red Flag*, the Party's journal, in August 1968. It was by Yao Wen-yuan, now a leading figure among the younger members of the CCP's upper echelons. 'The Working-class Must Exercise Leadership in Everything' came at a time when the Red Guards had ceased to be the admired shock troops and were divided by faction fights. The workers were to come to the rescue by entering and guiding all educational institutions.

The same article contains one of the more enthusiastic over-statements of the case! 'Workers can't understand education, say some so-called high-ranking intellectuals. Away with your ugly *bourgeois* intellectual airs. What you understand is the pseudo-knowledge of the *bourgeoisie*. Those who teach science and engineering don't know how to operate or repair machines; those who teach literature don't know how to write essays.'

It soon became clear that the younger intellectuals—and some older ones—were not to practise manual labour for short periods only, or even for a few years before their higher education. On graduation they were exhorted to go pioneering in the outback, to help develop backward rural areas using their education to help 'serve the people' and the country. *China Youth Daily* announced: 'Recently large numbers of educated youth have rushed to the countryside forming a new revolutionary current. . . Going to the rural and mountain areas, urban-educated youth have embarked upon a glorious revolutionary road, a road on which they can join the workers and peasants. They ask, "Is there a bright future ploughing the soil?" Our reply is, "Educated youths will have an endless bright and great future in rural and mountain areas".'

Many young city-dwellers found country life very tough going indeed, as an article in *China Pictorial* revealed. 'In 1964 Liang Hsiu-ying, a young woman intellectual, went proudly and enthusiastically to the agricultural front. At first with the young people chatting and joking she enjoyed it very much; but as time went on the renegade Liu Shao-chi's theory of "studying in order to climb up" cropped up again in her mind.

'After work one day, having dragged her weary body home, she tossed aside the hoe and threw herself on the bed complaining, "To think of a middle school graduate digging the earth all day long". From then on she had been preoccupied with leaving.'

In the end, after re-education by the peasants and long soul-searching Hsiu-ying 'comes good'. But clearly, many others would find it hard to do so. A young Canton college graduate who left for Hong Kong said his friends wrote to him of poor food, and accommodation and the suspicion of the peasants and local populace.

But many settled down in their new life as Western visitors have reported; China, it seems, will not be troubled by the too-common Asian problem of unemployed graduates walking city streets.

Western visitors also report that though the Cultural Revolution is over, many of the innovations it brought have come to stay. Education institutions are now controlled by 'revolutionary committees', old-style entrance examinations have been abolished and even the term 'intellectuals' for a separate class, may be on the way out.

R. L. Whitehead, an American educationist, described the governing body of Peking University: 'The Revolutionary Committee, formed in 1969, has . . . members elected by students, teachers and workers. Of these seven are from the PLA, six from workers' teams which come from off campus, six are cadres, seven students, nine faculty members, three representatives of workers in campus factories and one representative of staff families. There is also a Party Committee similarly organised.'[6]

Of equal importance is the now nation-wide method of selection for higher education. The 'three doors' picture is no more—from home to school; from school to college and from there to a safe job in teaching or the public service. All students, from primary school up, and their teachers, do practical work in workshops or factories on the premises or nearby. Selection for higher education comes after two or more years of working. Professor R. Frankenburg of Keele University in England visited Tsinghua University in Peking and discussed at length its recruitment policies. 'No longer do students come directly after examinations from middle schools. They come from production to learn to go back to production. The masses in the localities are asked to nominate suitable people who have worked for two or three years. There are five conditions that must normally be fulfilled. They must be adept in the living, study and application of Marxism-Leninism-Mao Tse-tung Thought; have practical experience; have been at middle school at least until sixteen and be twenty years old. They stay for two or three years with all expenses paid . . . They study production on the actual site . . . The university incorporates a motor vehicle plant, a provision factory and an electronic works.'

The Great Proletarian Cultural Revolution of the 1960s is over; but, says Mao, it is only the first: 'There will inevitably be more in the future. The issue of who will win the revolution can be settled only over a long historical period . . . It should not be thought . . by anyone in our country that everything will be all right after one or two great cultural revolutions, or even three or four.'

'Spiritual Aggression'. Old Entrance Gate, Peking University. 'Carrying on missionary activities, establishing hospitals and schools, publishing newspapers, and enticing Chinese students to study abroad, are the ways this policy is implemented. Their aim is to train intellectuals to serve their interests and to fool the great masses of the Chinese people.' (Mao Tse-tung)

Fudan University, Shanghai. 'In higher education the aim of reform was to rid the colleges and universities of courses with a reactionary content. Generally speaking the university professors were too conservative and were slow to consider present day needs.' (*China in Transition*)

Chinese scientists were the first in history to produce, in 1965, synthetic bovine crystalline insulin by chemical means. In 1971 they succeeded in determining the spatial structure of molecules of crystalline pig insulin. They did this using the method of X-ray diffraction at a resolution of $2 \cdot 5$ angstroms.

Yangtse Bridge, Nanking.

Tomb of Emperor Wan Li, one of the Ming tombs on the outskirts of Peking where emperors and queens of the Ming dynasty were buried.

Fankua Lane, Shanghai, as it was, and after redevelopment. It was reduced to rubble during the early period of the Anti-Japanese War and bamboo and matting huts were put up. These five-storey apartment buildings are modern and well lit.

Students of a cadre school reclaiming land from sandy waste and marshes. 'Traitor Liu Shao-chi did everything he could to spread reactionary fallacies such as that manual labour is inferior, officials are superior and the people are lowly. He argued that the aim of studying was personal prestige and manual labour a punishment for mistakes. His aim was to turn cadres into intellectual aristocrats divorced from proletarian politics, workers, peasants and from production. Cadres so corrupted can serve his scheme of capitalist restoration for China.' (*China Reconstructs*)

A factory worker explaining pulleys to third-grade students. 'It is imperative for us to carry forward our Party's tradition of keeping in close touch with the masses and working hard under all conditions. Leading cadres at all levels must participate in physical labour so as gradually to combine mental and physical work.' (Central Committee Directive, 1957)

'Mao has been surprisingly successful in his efforts to break down the old taboos against manual labour and the old barriers between the ruling class and the common man, between the intelllectuals and the workers and peasants.' (*Newsweek*, 21 February, 1972)

Workers' propaganda teams. 'The workers' propaganda teams are entering the fields of education. This is an earth-shaking event. Schools were the monopoly of the exploiting classes and their children from ancient times. Conditions improved somewhat after liberation but in the main schools were monopolised by *bourgeois* intellectuals. It is impossible for students and intellectuals alone to fulfill the tasks of struggle-criticism-transformation. Workers and PLA fighters must take part. The workers will not stay in the schools just for a few days; they will keep working there permanently and always occupy the school-front and lead the schools.' (*China Pictorial*)

A veteran worker lecturing students at Tsing[University. Professor Philip Huang of UCLA, instance, tells of attending a meeting at Peki Tsinghua University and hearing a thirty-t year old labourer assigned to campus mainten[discuss school problems with the university presi without the slightest trace of servility. An Chinese-American couple, Veronica and Ern Yhap, report that at a Chinese hospital visited everyone—doctors, nurses, orderli pitched in to prepare a patient's room.

Chou En-lai chatting with some of the educated young people from Shanghai working at the Shihhotzu Farm in the Sinkiang Uighur Autonomous Region. 'Many leaders in our Party Central Committee came from upper middle classes; those from worker and peasant families are very few. This did not hinder their becoming leaders of our Party.' (Chen Yi)

Chou and Chen Yi came from mandarin backgrounds, Mao and Liu from rich peasant families; all were well-educated.

A PLA fighter stands guard. 'Don't hit people; coercion or force in the struggle only touches people's skins. Only by reasoning is it possible to touch their hearts.' (Lin Piao, 1966)

Party and state leaders Liu Shao-chi, Chu
(left) and Peng Chen (right) at the Wor
People's Palace of Culture on May Day.

Peking Red Guards renaming East Yang
(displaying pomposity) Road, on which the So
Embassy is located, as Fanhsiu (anti-revision
Road.

Students of Peking Teachers' University; a
Guards dance group.

Red Guards propagating Mao Tsetung Thought on the street.

'Our great leader, Chaiman Mao, spent more than six hours with the revolutionary masses that morning [in Tien Anmen Square]. Side by side with Comrade Lin Piao he reviewed the one million strong army of the Great Proletarian Cultural Revolution. During the rally a Red Guard from the Girls' Middle School attached to Peking Normal University, mounted the rostrum and put a red armband of the Red Guards on Chairman Mao. One thousand five hundred student representatives mounted the rostrum.' (*China Pictorial*)

16 The Intellectual and the Revolutionary Tradition

It was the special genius of Mao Tse-tung, peasant-born intellectual, which combined for the first time the two main streams of Chinese revolutionary history and led their representatives to victory at a time when China's fortunes had reached their nadir. The quotations show he was well aware of China's famous teachers of the past to whose legacy he was heir, and he was aware, too, of the contribution of academics to the reform and revolutionary movements of the nineteenth and early twentieth centuries. But he realised also the dangers of the intellectual tradition and all his life has struggled against these while seeking to harness the intellectuals for what he saw as the national good. He recalls his own early attitudes at the Yenan Forum in 1942: 'If you want to be understood by and identified with the people, you must make up your mind to undergo a long and even painful process of remoulding.

'As a student I used to feel it undignified to do any manual labour, such as carrying my own luggage in the presence of a crowd of fellow students who could not fetch and carry for themselves. The revolution brought me into the ranks of the workers, peasants and soldiers in the revolutionary army, and gradually I became familiar with them and they with me. It was then and only then that a fundamental change occurred in the *bourgeois* and *petit-bourgeois* feelings implanted in me by the *bourgeois* schools. I came to feel that the unremoulded intellectuals were unclean as compared with the workers and peasants who are the cleanest people, cleaner than the *bourgeois* and *petit-bourgeois* intellectuals, even though their hands are blackened by work and their feet smeared with cow dung.'

And he commented later: 'The ideological reform of the intellectuals is one of the important conditions for our country's all-out, complete democratic reform.'

Mao was born in 1893 in Shaoshan village, Hunan province, his father being classed as a rich peasant, though only very moderately well-off. At his primary school the students were forced to memorise the classics regardless of whether or not they understood them. He became an omnivorous reader with a special taste for the classical legends of rebel heroes as, for example, 'The Water Margin' and 'The Romance of the Three Kingdoms'. In his late teens he met, for the first time, foreign periodicals and the famous translations by Yen Fu of Western political books and treatises. He read historical biographies, being especially impressed by Napoleon, Washington and Lincoln. After shifting about rather restlessly and spending some time in the then revolutionary army and some on his father's farm, Mao settled for school-teaching as a career and spent from 1913 to 1918 at the First Teachers' Training School in Changsha where his essays were regularly displayed as model exercises. He helped found the New People's Study Society and contributed an article to the *Hunan Critic*, 'The Great Union of the Popular Masses', which caused discussion even in faraway Peking; it was his first adumbration of his philosophy of the power of the 'masses', the 'people'; these should consist of the united peasants, workers, students and—significantly—women. The *Hunan Critic* was only one of a spate of papers directing scathing criticism at the traditional Confucian ethic, the patriarchal tradition and the education system. The best-known was *New Youth* (*La Jeunesse*), which first appeared in 1915.

After graduating in 1918 Mao found a very minor job in the Peking

University library where he met the famous revolutionary scholar, Li Ta-chao. Through him he discovered Marxism and also the ambivalence of the contribution of the intellectuals to China's reform and revolutionary movements. They had started the ferment of inquiry and roused the people to China's plight but many, growing fearful of the power they had roused, later retreated from the struggle or even opposed it.

The reform movements started with China's defeat by the Western powers; the realisation of the inferiority of the great Middle Kingdom. 'The fundamental reason for the defeat of the Chinese in the Opium War was our backwardness. Our troops were an anachronism, our government mediaeval, and our people, including the official class, have a mediaeval mentality. There was no mystery in our defeat; it was inevitable,' commented Tsiang Ting-fu, KMT diplomat, in the 1930s.

The traditional examination system, centuries old, was one of the institutions most scathingly condemned. It was seen as an arid, time-wasting series of formal exercises in futility, diverting abilities from constructive activity. Yet it was through this system that official promotion lay.

One of the most influential scholars at the turn of the century was Kang Yu-wei, who actually managed to persuade the young emperor, Kuang Hsu, to initiate a programme of reform. It lasted barely three months—The Hundred Days of Reform—for the formidable Empress Dowager intervened and swept both reform and emperor briskly into the discard. Kang Yu-wei fled; he gave up the unequal struggle and was to end his days as the very symbol of traditional China. One of his pupils, the brilliant Liang Chi-chao, had a not dissimilar career. In his writings and teaching he made a notable contribution to the development of a national consciousness, but, by the Communists, he is regarded as a lost leader, not a true revolutionary. As a young man he declared, 'Self-government is the basis of progress: The old must go, by peaceful means as in Japan, or by violence. Change, destruction, is inevitable whether one wills it or not. If reform is obstructed revolution is inevitable.' He moved from reform to revolution and then back to reform, finally finishing up as a strong opponent to Sun Yat-sen before fading into obscurity. Another famous scholar, Chang Chih-tung in his *Exhortation to Study*, stated categorically: 'The doctrine of people's rights can bring us not a single benefit but a hundred evils.'

Sun Yat-sen commented bitterly on the antagonism of the intellectuals, but one group of them rallied to his support; the influential Japan-educated graduates, many imbued with revolutionary fervour, flocked to hear and encourage Sun when he spoke in Tokyo. On their return home many of them became major agitators, and many lost their lives in abortive uprisings. One student in Japan was Wu Yu-chang, later a member of the CCP Central Committee; his book, *The Revolution of 1911*, gives a valuable first-hand account of intellectual activities at this period.

Two of the most admired intellectuals, reformers and revolutionaries alike, in the 1920s and 1930s were the author, Lu Hsun, and the Peking University scholar, Chen Tu-hsiu, who wrote a stirring call to youth: 'Oh, young men of China! Will you be able to understand me? Five out of every ten whom I see are young in age, but old in spirit . . . When this happens to a body, the body is dying. When it happens to a society, the society is perishing. Such a sickness cannot be cured by sighing in words; it can only be cured by those who are young, and in addition to being young, are courageous . . . We must have youth if we are to survive, we must have youth if we are to get rid of corruption. Here lies the hope for our society.'

Chen became secretary of the Communist Party and wielded considerable influence but was later discredited.

Regarded by both Nationalist and Communist Chinese as crucial, the May Fourth Movement started in Peking University when the terms of the Versailles Treaty became known in 1919. Protest spread like wildfire through the country. The intelligentsia and small merchant class of China, more than most countries, had hoped for a new spirit of international affairs after World War I and Woodrow Wilson's promises, but when the news of the peace conference reached them, they were disillusioned.[1] So many students were arrested that the prisons could not hold them. Most were set free. The establishment condemned the movement but its influence was great among scholars and *bourgeoisie*.

More fiercely than ever raged the reform or revolution debate. Said Li Ta-chao: 'Behold, the world of the future; it is the world of the Red Flag.' For Mao, 'The May Fourth Movement came into being at the call of the Russian Revolution of Lenin'.

To the lower intellectuals the whole Westernised élite, as represented by scholar and writer Hu Shih, for example, seemed politically weak; they left the field open to more emphatic doctrines from the left.

'Finally I struck on the truth which would really bring salvation. It was the universal truth . . . of Marxism-Leninism. The victory of the October Revolution in 1917 illuminated the correct road for the people of the world; it was under its resplendent light that the May Fourth Movement was launched and in July 1921 the CCP was founded,' wrote Wu Yu-chang.

In the *Communist International* of October 1936, Chen Pan-tsu, who was present at the occasion, gives a unique account of the now-famous CCP's First Congress which met in, of all places, a girls' school in the French Concession of Shanghai. (It was vacation-time, of course!)

Virtually all thirteen members present, and most of the other Party members unable to attend, belonged to the 'learned elements'. Many, indeed the majority, did not stay the revolutionary course, some even going over to the 'Chiang clique' and becoming actively anti-Party. The record helps to explain the continuing wariness of the Communist Party towards the intelligentsia. Liu Jen-ching was expelled from the Party as a Trotskyist and joined the KMT police; Chen Tu-hsiu, one-time Party secretary, was later discredited as a rightist, Pao Hui-sheng is now regarded as a renegade—he and other leaders of the Returned Students' Group (i.e. from Japan) became Mao's rivals and critics.

The problem of where to place the intellectuals and *bourgeois* continues to crop up repeatedly throughout subsequent CCP conferences. Mao returns often to the problem of their place in the whole revolutionary movement. 'The Sixth Congress of the CCP (1928) failed to work out a correct estimate of the dual character of the intermediate classes . . . it considered the national *bourgeoisie* "one of the most dangerous enemies that hinder the victory of the revolution" ignoring the dual character of the national *bourgeoisie*. It failed to see the possibility of a change in the political attitude of this class.' Again, in 1939, Mao shows the same concern: 'Many cadres in the army are not aware of the importance of the intellectuals and are still afraid of them or even desire to keep them out of the ranks. This arises from a failure to understand the importance of the intellectuals to the revolutionary cause. All Party organisations should draw in large numbers of intellectuals to join our army and schools and work in our government. Thus the workers and peasant cadres can become intellectuals while the intellectuals can acquire the good qualities of the worker and the peasant classes.'

The May Thirtieth Incident took place in 1925. Most Chinese historians today regard the date as more important than May 4, since the student demonstrators received far more massive support from the workers and middle-class—the 'national *bourgeoisie*'. The violent reaction of the British police in the concession area inflamed and united public opinion throughout the country.

During the early 1930s Mao was in eclipse and little is heard of him in Party records; he was even deprived of his voting rights. The Returned Scholars, Chen Tu-hsiu and Chang Kou-tao, could not accept Mao's peasant-line and were suspicious of workers' action. Chen is accused of trying to hinder strikes in the cities, supporting the 'Li Li-san line' of direct attacks against key cities which met, as we have seen, with disastrous losses. Mao later accused them of dogmatism and empiricism. 'How can we turn these intellectuals who have only book knowledge into real intellectuals? The only way is to make them take part in practical work.'

In 1935 at Tsunyi, Kweichow Province, while on the Long March, Mao was elected Chairman of the Party and thereafter retained unquestioned leadership in spite of many attacks and, as the revelations of the Cultural Revolution indicated, some bitter opposition from former close colleagues. But Mao's philosophic imprint was there and the masses were Mao's masses. However, they were not to make revolution alone an isolated class. They were to combine with other revolutionary classes. Marxism-Leninism differentiates between the democratic revolution and the Socialist revolution which follows it and, said Mao, a 'clear understanding of the differences and interconnections is indispensible to correct leadership. . . . The proletariat, the peasantry and the intelligentsia and the other sections of the *petit bourgeois*, undoubtedly constitute the basic forces determining China's fate. These classes will become the basic components of the state and governmental structure . . . with the proletariat as the leading force.

'The Chinese democratic republic . . . must be under the joint dictatorship of all anti-imperialist, anti-feudal people led by the proletariat . . . we Communists must never push aside anyone who is revolutionary, we shall persevere in the united front and practise long-term co-operation [with such classes].'

After Tsunyi the Red Army pressed on, reaching journey's end in the bleak hills of Shensi Province where they settled in the loess caves and huts of Yenan. Here, for nearly a decade, the Communists were to remain and Mao was to write his most influential treatises. Here his colleagues, men of powerful intellects and capacities, Chou En-lai, Chen Yi, Chu Teh, Lin Piao and Liu Shao-chi, planned in minute detail the future organisation and administration of the united China that was to be theirs. Mao's Yenan works include *On Practice*, *On Contradiction*, *On the New Democracy*, *On Protracted War* and *On the Chinese Revolution and the CCP*, as well as the *Forum on Literature and the Arts*.

The Yenan period proper is almost synonymous with the Anti-Japanese War, the course of which was greatly determined by Mao's military writings—now classics of their kind. He differentiated between mobile, guerrilla and positional warfare and prophesied three main phases of the struggle; 1. The Japanese strategic offensive and the Reds' defensive; 2. The Japanese strategic consolidation and the Reds' preparation for counter-offensive; 3. The Reds' strategic offensive and the Japanese retreat. Above all, there was to be no haste, no direct attack on the cities as the Li Li-san line had so disastrously demanded; the countryside would surround the cities until they were ready to be taken by the People's Liberation Army.

Mao was not writing in isolation in his cave in the Date Garden. Yenan became a centre of activity, a creative force whose influence spread wide. After months of negotiations the National government reluctantly recognised the Border Areas (the Liberated Areas, to the Communists) and the Red Army became the Eighth Route Army. The American General Peabody, writing in 1944, estimated that by 1937 the Party controlled about 35 000 square miles with a population of about a million and a half, which, six years later, had expanded to some quarter of a million square miles with about eighty-five million people. In spite of very stringent KMT blockades the existence of such a region could not wholly be kept quiet; indeed Yenan's fame spread, not least the fame of its Anti-Japanese Military and Political Institute, Kangta, for short, staffed by scholars and teachers who had found their way to Yenan from every part of the country.

Along with a few other Western intellectuals Professor William Band made a hazardous journey from Peking, where he taught physics at the university, to the Border Region and Kangta. He certainly grasped Mao's message! 'Since attending the first science congress in the Border District, June 1942 . . . one thing has been driven home to me. We intellectuals have lived in our own world cut off completely from the real life of the nation . . . But at last we have discovered true intellectuals without class feeling, false pride or intellectual snobbery. We are all confident of victory and we are all going back to Peking; but are we going back to our old ways, our old scramble for PhD's and professorships? No! A thousand times no! The New China will need all the scientists she can produce . . . and they must realise their responsibilities towards the millions of peasants who are the backbone of Chinese ancient and modern culture.'[2]

Since Chiang Kai-shek continued to enforce rigid blockades of the Border Region, almost all supplies of food, clothing, military materials and medical supplies—many sent by China's allies and by the international agencies such as the Red Cross—failed to reach the Red guerrillas and the Border Regions, civilians there had to make an unending effort to keep people fed, clothed and fit. The army became a production as well as a fighting force and every student and teacher, woman and child joined them in this. Stuart Gelder gives his eyewitness account of the success of this campaign, also this extract from the Regions' Annual Report, 1943. 'One small unit cultivated 1 725 mou of land (about 287 acres) produced [hundreds of pounds] of foodstuffs, vegetables and hay. In addition they chopped tons of firewood, manufactured or purchased 13 000 tools of production and engaged in stock-breeding, handicrafts and transport . . . They have reached the goal of "abundant clothing and sufficient food". They have had harvests in cotton, hemp, tobacco, melons and fruits. In production as in fighting our troops are very active. Last Spring they went up to the hills before dawn and remained until after dusk and worked in the recess allowed them after each meal. This compelled the commanders to lay down a rule that no one shall start before worktime or remain after it.'

At this time the New Zealand journalist, James Bertram, had an interview with Mao. 'Mao struck me as having incomparably the coolest and most balanced mind that I had encountered in China. Talking to him one is immediately aware of an immense intellectual force, a brain moving easily and surely along orderly lines of thought. This penetrating intelligence is combined with an essentially practical approach to any problem and a deep understanding of his own countrymen.'[3]

Throughout the Border Regions land-reform, initiated as we saw in the Kiangsi Soviets in the early 1930s, was continued, at first fairly gradually, then with increasing speed and thoroughness. Intellectuals from schools and colleges took part, William Hinton, author of *Fanshen*, among them. 'The Northern University, the educational centre of the Shansi-Honan-Hopei-Shantung Border Region, was a guerrilla institution which moved according to the dictates of war. I had no sooner settled there than half the faculty and students departed to join the land reform movement. [A girl student from a wealthy family was in the party.]

'I often thought what hardship it must be for such a woman to live the Spartan life of a revolutionary cadre in the bleak North China countryside. Yet she seemed to pay no attention to cold, fatigue, lice, fleas . . . or the hard wooden planks that served as her bed. Her high spirits in the face of extreme physical hardship pointed up a curious fact . . . the morale of the intellectuals for whom land reform represented a complete change in way of life was far higher than that of the local cadres. They plunged into the heart of village affairs with eagerness . . . I never saw one complain.'

An integral and uniquely Chinese part of the great land reforms were the Talk Bitterness meetings. Mary Endicott, a Canadian author, quotes a Chinese scholar's account of such a meeting. 'When they feel the collective strength that is generated from organising such a number to meet together they are ready to hold their first "suffering meeting". Families come and sit in groups; then, with some encouragement . . . the peasants begin to tell what they have suffered. Our Chinese term for it means to "talk bitterness". Slowly at first, then with greater detail and more rush of feeling, one after another rises and tells how the landlord demanded the full quota of the crop from him even when there was a drought. How he increased the quota till he hadn't enough left for his children and they starved to death . . . And then, as the people realised that at last they could speak out and the landlord could not take revenge on them, they would pour out terrible stories of rape, murder, and torture. Down their honest faces . . . the tears would come in a flood . . . All of us wept with them . . . No one took notes of what was said in these meetings. None would be held to account for his testimony, for this was not a court. They were free to tell it all, and they had no need to exaggerate, for the truth was bad enough and each knew from his own sufferings that what the others said was true. We who had come from outside knew it was true, because the same kind of stories had been poured out in such meetings all over China . . . It was a deeply moving experience for us as well as for the peasants. One sees in these meetings and in the whole method in which Land Reform is carried out how deeply the roots of this new order are found in the people themselves—the true meaning of democracy.'[4]

But land-reform, the manner and extent of it, raised immense problems for peasants, intellectuals and Party leaders alike. After the victory against Japan, when civil war loomed and broke, the peasants had to make up their minds whether or not to stay with the Reds to resist the mighty Nationalist offensive. As for the educated cadres, they had similar problems, as Hinton tells us. 'Many of them were landlords' sons and daughters standing on the revolutionary side because it had fought the Japanese . . . They had to decide if they would opt for land reform, which alone could mobilise the peasantry, at a time when support for land reform meant throwing down the gauntlet, initiating a life and death struggle with the KMT for state power . . . in a land already torn by eight years of war . . . The debate split the Central Committee of the CCP.'[5]

As Hinton goes on to explain, the real question was who would hold on to the gun out of whose barrel all power grows; that is who would maintain control of the Eighth Route Army? The Cultural Revolution revealed the complexity of the decision and the role of Liu Shao-chi and other leaders who urged limited land-reform and compromise with the KMT, maybe even a coalition government.

In the end it was the peasants, roused and militant, who took the issue out of the hands of intellectual cadres and Central Committee alike. The masses—the proletarian leaders—had decided, and Mao was with them. The Second Civil War, the War of Liberation, had started, as massive land-reform action began and landlords went on trial everywhere.

Both in the country and in the cities and small towns, life went on with increasing difficulties in the areas under the weakening control of a Nationalist government growing ever more corrupt and disorganised and thrashing out wildly against critics in its panic. In the streets thousands starved, millions went hungry. Again the intellectuals and all the *petit bourgeois* suffered bitterly. Almost every college-and middle school throughout the country was a centre for bitter criticism of the Nationalist government; the middle class sympathised and joined them in demonstrations and often violent protest. All were ruthlessly suppressed.

William Sewell writes movingly of his own experiences on his campus in Szechuan: 'In 1939 rice cost two Chinese dollars a bushel . . . in 1941 it had risen to $45. In 1948 it cost $110 000. Paper money was worthless; we were millionaires but unable to cope . . .

When the news flashed by that salaries could be drawn we stopped classes and ran to the shops with prepared lists. How our servant survived I did not know until I discovered he had sold his daughter to a brothel. The students I knew had, on several occasions, eaten dog for their supper. It seemed to be generally accepted that even a mangy street dog could be eaten with some satisfaction if properly cooked. . . Rumours came to the university that Chiang, before leaving, had ordered all political prisoners to be killed; nearly all three hundred were shot or buried alive in Chungking. Would the same thing happen in our prison? . . . May-lan came to tell me, "They have dug up the bodies—twenty in all. Some were stabbed in the back—others had no wounds but there was blood from nose and ears. They were buried alive." We stood, not saying a word; in the mind of each of us the same thought. Chang Er-mi, our senior student, who had been arrested! It was true. He had been killed without trial.'[6]

A few families, the Soongs and Kungs among them, were multi-millionaires (in foreign currency), but most educated and formerly moderately prosperous families were in desperate straits, which became increasingly worse as the 1940s drew to a close. Even anti-Communist Western observers abandoned hope in the Nationalist government's ability to mitigate the suffering—let alone end it. And they knew that millions were looking to the Communists at least for some kind of relief. The position was especially clear and particularly disturbing for Americans whose government and taxpayers were financing most of Chiang's war effort. US Ambassador Bullett and US General Wedemeyer wrote home the same story in 1947: 'The bulk of the people are not disposed towards Communism . . . [but accept it] in an indignant protest against oppressive police measures, corrupt practices, and maladministration of National officials . . . and their reactionary leadership, oppression and corruption.' Professor Dirk Bodde reported in his *Peking Diary* a conversation he had in 1948 with a Chinese colleague in Peking. 'We have become so completely convinced of the hopelessness of the existing government that we feel the sooner it is removed the better. Since the Chinese communists are obviously the only force capable of making this change we are now willing to support them as the lesser of two evils. We ourselves would prefer a middle course but this is no longer possible.'

Indeed, a middle course was no longer possible for Chiang. On the battle front between 1945 and 1949 the fight was to be fought to its bitter finish, and many of the intellectuals and middle class knew, as well as the peasants, what the result would be, though they may not have admitted it even to themselves.

The Empress Dowager repudiating the petition
for reform.

Emperor Kuang Hsu.

The Empress Dowager Tzu Hsi and her ladies.

Examination supervisor's tower. 'All China-str
bound books [i.e. those printed before the imp
of the West] should be thrown into the toilet a
not read for thirty years.' (Wu Chih-hui)

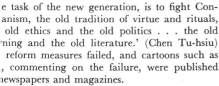

Cartoon lampooning the shortage of student accommodation. 'A classroom like this is as rare as a phoenix.'

e task of the new generation, is to fight Con-anism, the old tradition of virtue and rituals, old ethics and the old politics . . . the old rning and the old literature.' (Chen Tu-hsiu) reform measures failed, and cartoons such as , commenting on the failure, were published ewspapers and magazines.

May Fourth movement. 'The universities were under military guard. More than two thousand ents were arrested. Throughout the whole of na a general strike of students took place . . . government, fearing a *coup d'etat*, was obliged t all the students free, expel two ministers and storm was temporarily calmed.' (Student paper , *East Asian History*, no. 2, Columbia University) eneral Chiang Chi-ching thought the students' duct irresponsible and 'degenerate'. Professor n Dewey wrote in Peking: 'We have just seen ew hundred girls marched away from the erican mission school to go see the President ask him to release the boy students who are rison for making speeches in the street. . . . We witnessing the birth of a nation and birth always es hard.'

'In May 1925 . . . the management of a Japan
mill in Shanghai killed a worker and woun
more than ten others. Thereupon the stude
started a campaign on 30 May, and rallied m
than ten thousand people in the British concessi
The British police opened fire, killing and wound
many students. This massacre immediately arou
nation-wide demonstrations . . . and strikes
workers, students and shopworkers.' (Chin
historian)

The Nationalist government's failure to halt Japa
increasing encroachments into China arou
students to another demonstration, in Decem
1935. 'Stop the Civil War', 'Unite to Resist Japa
read their placards. They were savagely trea
by the authorities.

Sun Yat-sen as a student, second from left. He a
his three friends were known as 'the four a
rebels'. 'The intellectuals regard me as a ban
an unprincipled man, guilty of treason . . . a
poisonous snake or a wild animal.'

...angsha Normal School. 'I was a student at a ...rmal School for five years. Incidents in my life ...e . . . were many and during this period my ...itical ideas began to take shape. Here also I ...quired my first experiences in social action. . . . ...that time it seemed to me that the intellectuals ...ne were clean while the workers and peasants ...re rather dirty. I could put on the clothes of other ...ellectuals because I thought them clean, but ...uld not put on clothes belonging to a worker ...peasant because I thought them dirty.' (Mao ...-tung)

The Peasant Movement Training Institute, Canton, where Mao taught in 1925–6. In this period he wrote his famous treaties, *Analysis of the Classes in Chinese Society*, 1926, and *Report on the Peasant Movement in Hunan*, 1927.

Mao on the way to take part in the big strike at the Anyuan Collieries, 1922. This portrait was painted by a group of art students during the Cultural Revolution.

aoshan, Mao's birthplace.

Outside the meeting place; the meeting room where the first National Congress of the Chinese Communist Party began, and the memorial boat (a reproduction) at Nanhu. 'Altogether thirteen delegates attended the conference. On the fourth day after supper . . . about 8 o'clock a suspicious person in a long coat appeared. . . . He explained he was looking for the Chairman of the Association of Social Organisations, Wan by name, and that he was mistaken and speedily left. . . . His appearance seemed suspicious so we gathered together our papers and disappeared. Only two stayed behind and before ten minutes had passed nine spies and policemen turned up and began to search the apartment.' The work of the Congress was concluded on a holiday boat hired, ostensibly, for a few days' vacation. (Communist International, October 1936)

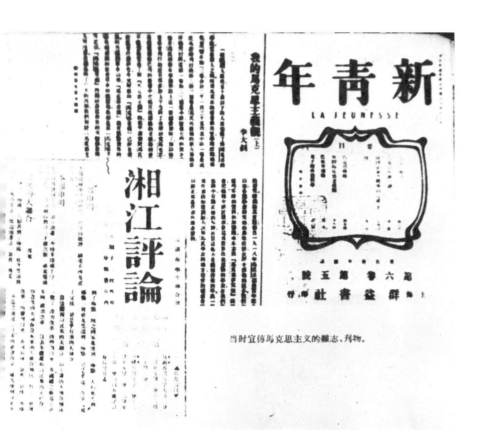

当时宣传马克思主义的杂志、刊物。

…na Youth, (La Jeunesse), an early revolutionary
…gazine.

Juichin in Kiangsi Province. The meeting hall of
the first Chinese Soviet government, 1927–8.

Tsunyi. 'When Chiang Kai-shek gathered a million troops and 200 aeroplanes to launch the fifth counter-revolutionary campaign "of encirclement and suppression", the Red Army in the central revolutionary area fought valiantly but failed to defeat the enemy because the Wang Ming opportunist line had negated Chairman Mao's leadership of the Party and his command of the army, and a wrong political and military line had been put into effect. . . . The conference of the Party's Central Committee . . . convened at Tsunyi in Kweichow Province, corrected the existing military and organisational mistakes and established a new leadership headed by Comrade Mao Tse-tung.' (*China Pictorial*)

Iron smelting: 'The masses of peasantry . . . schools, the government organisations, ha carried on a production campaign for a wh year; they are mobilised into a labour army witho exception. Thus besides an army for fighting have an army for production.'

inning: 'When we entered the Communist areas
e expected to see the people hanging on grimly
 the face of economic blockade of their barren
rderland. We found instead that the cultivation
s more extensive than in any other part of
rth-west China, the people were better fed and
tter dressed and a certain amount of industry
d developed. . . . The peasants have come to
ow 60 per cent of the region's requirements.'
he Chinese Communists, by Stuart Gelder)

'speak bitterness' meeting of the Red Army.

'Hundreds of volunteers joined equal numbers of local cadres [trained persons playing a role in any area of political activity]. . . . In groups of ten or twelve they were to go out to survey the true conditions of the peasant population and help to carry land reform through to completion. The excitement generated by the departure of so many students and staff members electrified the whole university. Many who had not been chosen to go stood around with wistful expressions.' (*Fanshen*, by William Hinton)

All Chinese, but especially the intellectuals, bitterly resented the influence and arrogance of the 'occupying powers'. In the concession areas in Shanghai, Western ways were dominant and Chinese treated as second-class citizens. The famous infamous 'Chinese and Dogs Forbidden' park-notice typified the attitude of West towards East. In China a few Chinese sought to forget their own traditions and assume Western dress and style of living.

'A Chinese dandy', a cartoon dated 1903. 'Some sixty thousand foreigners were living in the twelve square miles of the two foreign municipalities. Nearly twenty thousand were refugee Russians who "didn't count"; 20 000 were Japanese who kept to themselves. Of the remaining 20 000, nine were British, four American, and two and a half French. . . . The British style of life prevailed. Most of the do's and don'ts were British and a good many Americans were absorbed by Shanghai's British atmosphere.' (*Shanghai in 1930*, by O. E. Hauser)

During the inflation panic of December 1948, thousands of Shanghai citizens besieged the Kuomintang's Central Bank of China to exchange paper currency for gold.

n inflation clerk: 'It was impossible to live on one's ages as the depreciation of the currency took place om hour to hour or even from minute to minute. 1948 a lunch at the Palace Hotel, Shanghai, cost illions of Chinese dollars. Soup was $800 000 and icken liver with mushrooms $3 500 000.' (*America d China*, by Professor Chang Hsin-hai)

hiang's war was financed at the cost of the middle ass and by the reduction of the standard of living such fixed income groups as school teachers, ofessors, government employees. The cost of ing today [1947] is approximately thirty ousand times what it was in 1936. The middle ass is ruined.' (Report of US Ambassador William llitt)

he personal fortunes accumulated by the four big milies, Chiang Kai-shek, Foreign Minister H. H. ung, Finance Minister T. V. Soong and the en brothers were estimated at $US20 000 illion.

Police hosing student demonstrators.

Demonstration in Taiwan in 1947 against the Nationalist government. People of Taipei set fire to the warehouse of the KMT Commodity Monopoly Bureau.

Chinese Communist Party offices in Yenan.

It is likely that future historians will divide the period of the People's Republic of China into two phases: before and after the Great Proletarian Cultural Revolution of 1966–8. In many respects social conditions differ in these two periods, and much of what was correctly reported of the first phase does not now apply to the second. In the early period the régime sought to recruit the intellectuals to its service by offering them reasonably well-paid employment in activity which used their skills and knowledge, gave them security, and a standard of living not much inferior to that which they had enjoyed before the Japanese invasion, and very much better than that to which they had been reduced by the invasion and subsequent civil war. Land reform, leading step by step to the communes, had revolutionised the situation of the peasants even more profoundly, but the distinction between urban worker and peasant farmer was still clear enough, and as workers by 'brain' were ranked equal to workers by hand, the urban working class included, nominally at least, the intellectuals. These educated people did not, of course, share the experiences and outlook of former poor peasants or urban workers. Much of their thinking and aspirations were still attached to the old values of the culture in which they had been brought up, a fact which was recognised, and even accepted by the Communist Party leadership at that time. There was a political party, in coalition with the Communist Party, called the Reform League, which had originally tried to oppose the Kuomintang dictatorship after the Japanese war. Crushed by Chiang Kai-shek, it had associated itself with the Communists at the time of their victory and became the recognised mouthpiece of the intellectuals, academic and professional class. Equally, the 'Revolutionary Kuomintang', a splinter of the left wing of the old Kuomintang, was admitted to the coalition and was assigned the task of representing the 'national *bourgeoisie*'—that is, the capitalist and merchant class who remained, under strict control, operating their plants and businesses in the great cities.

It remains uncertain and a matter of controversy whether this social pattern was expected to endure for some generations, or slowly wither away, or whether it was simply a stage which was a temporary convenience, to be eliminated in due course. It seems probable that opinion in the higher ranks of the Party was never unanimous on this question, and that the origin of the disputes during the Cultural Revolution lies in this difference. In the earlier phase social policy toward the class of *bourgeois* origin—by which is meant all those who were neither peasant farmers nor urban industrial or craft workers—was moderate and tolerant. Large capitalists and great merchants who chose to remain in China under the new régime were permitted to earn a five per cent dividend on the profits of their enterprises which they managed under a system of state–private partnership, in conjunction with officials of the régime. This system has some strong resemblances to the *Kuan-Shang*, 'Official and Merchant', system of managing large scale industries which had been operated from time to time under the imperial dynasties of the past. Such 'national capitalists' could still live in their large town houses, have their motor cars, and a way of life which, if not extravagant, was still very comfortable and undoubtedly *bourgeois*. Intellectuals and academics lived well also; it was normal to find that a professor or other higher professional man had a servant to cook in his home, and the use of a car for business purposes was also common. The schools attended by their children were the best, but were also preferred by the members of the Party hierarchy.

The system encouraged talent, and rewarded meritorious service with good pay and living conditions. Education was free from primary school to university, but the entrance requirements for each successive step up the ladder were very strict and narrow. Only the most talented could reach the university, where the idea of a 'failure rate' was an unknown concept. Those who had the benefit of education in the best schools and the background of an educated family home had a very real advantage. This came to mean the re-appearance of a new élite class, the educated, whether of *bourgeois* social origin, or of Party hierarch lineage; it was claimed during the Cultural Revolution that the system was thus gradually reintroducing and emphasising *bourgeois* values, and excluding from its greatest benefits the mass of the people. The fact that private property was reduced to the ownership of a single house (in a city or town) and a modest investment of savings in a government loan—no real estate in the country remaining in private hands—might appear to be a realisation of the Socialist policy in the economic field. But it did not really touch the system of privileges which were obtained by talent, aided by selective education, and sometimes, no doubt, by family influence. It was claimed by Mao Tse-tung in the Cultural Revolution that whereas the political revolution had been achieved by the 'War of Liberation' (the civil war from 1946-9) and the economic revolution achieved by the land reform and reform of the capitalist and commercial worlds in the early days of the People's Republic, there had as yet been no revolution touching the thinking of the nation, no change in the cultural values which came from the past, and a certain tendency for these values and ways of thought to reassert themselves under new forms. This is what is meant by 'revisionism', the fault found in many of the leaders of the Party who were driven from office during the Cultural Revolution.

That event, the full consequences of which cannot yet be assessed, radically changed the directives which Chinese society receives from its leaders. The ideal of the career open to talent, which would be duly rewarded on a scale well above the common standard, has been cast away. All must serve, according to their ability, but should expect no greater reward than is received by those with humbler skills. Privileges are under constant attack and suspicion. Even the use of cars by Party officials during the Cultural Revolution was often criticised and sometimes violently terminated. The 'national capitalists' no longer have their assured position, and it would seem that many of them have given up their dividends, or been induced to do so. Intellectuals of *bourgeois* origin are not now accorded any special treatment, and very many have been sent to remote country districts to employ their skills directly in the service of the peasant population of a commune. A determined attempt has been made to create a truly egalitarian society, rooting out all the vestiges of the old class structure which had survived, or revived. That this movement has won the support of the mass of the nation, who were not privileged nor particularly talented, cannot be doubted; that it may have some unexpected and perhaps undesirable results on the quality of the talent available in the next generation is a real possibility.

To remove and alter the entire class structure of an ancient society and prevent any tendency to revert to earlier patterns is a very difficult task. The old Chinese society, moreover, was not a strictly caste-segregated one, which once breached must open up a new line of development. By earlier standards the Chinese social system was a relatively open one, far more so than pre-modern Europe or most of Asia. For more than two thousand years there had not been an aristocracy in the real sense of the word in China, no class of hereditary nobility based on vast land holdings or vested right to govern. The family of the emperor bore titles; no one else held anything more than purely honorary ranks. The ruling class were the civil servants, the imperial bureaucracy, who were recruited from the educated class. This class came from the landed gentry, the owners of most of the best land, but not the exclusive owners of all of it. Landed estates were small, and usually made up of many parcels of small holdings, which were let out to tenants, and rents were high and harsh. Unlike the landed gentry of Europe the Chinese landlords rarely lived on their estates, but in a nearby city, large or small. This had not been the case in antiquity, nor perhaps until the late middle ages, but it was the rule for the past several centuries. The landlord was thus a countryman for his economic support, but an urban resident in his way of life. It was a bad development, which emphasised the unjust character of the land system. From the more talented members of such families the civil servants, the real rulers of China, were selected by severe and repeated public examinations, which except in periods of extreme dynastic decadence were strictly conducted and without favour or falsification of results.

Thus, although the old classification made no distinction between the types of 'scholar gentry' there was in fact a very real one; the distinction between the rich and the poor; those who could, by wealth, acquire a good education and the chance to compete for the civil service, and, if they succeeded, use wealth and influence to rise in the imperial service; and those who lacking the money to educate their children to this level were content to educate them to read and write, in the hope that these attainments would secure them minor posts in the public administration or in business. To read and to write, in the old society, meant not mere literacy, but ability to read the classical language, and to compose documents in it. The poorer gentry were becoming a depressed class in the last age of the empire. When the first revolution abolished the civil service examinations and the old system of education, substituting university education, they could not afford this new opening, and in many cases turned to the army, now the real holders of power, for careers and influence. Therefore Chiang's Kuomintang army was officered by men of small landlord status. Another solution, for the able, was to enter the educational world, now greatly expanding, and seek an academic career.

A similar distinction existed within the class of 'peasants', between free holders and tenants, or landless labourers. The Communists were to fasten upon this to create the categories 'rich, middle and poor peasants'. The merchant class was in the old category rated third (sometimes even fourth), but the reality here too was different, and far from uniform. There were very rich men, mainly in the great cities and particularly since the opening to China of foreign trade.

There were also moderately prosperous merchants and shop owners; and there were the really poor itinerant peddlers, or small stall-keepers— all classed as 'merchants'. Clearly their economic condition was diverse, and their educational standards ranged from highly culti-vated to wholly illiterate.

The real situation among the fourth class of the old category, the artisans, was equally unlike the official picture. There were, from many centuries past, very highly skilled silk workers, potters, carvers of jade and workers in both precious and utilitarian metals. There were also less skilled craftsmen in a wide range of occupations, and at the bottom, there were the day labourers, the 'coolies', who by 'bitter strength' (as the word *Ku li*, coolie, implies) gained a bare subsistence as long as their strength lasted. The skilled craftsmen were usually literate if not classically educated, the medium range could read and write and keep their accounts. In education, a large proportion of the urban working class were better educated than the peasants, and lived better also. Those at the bottom were more miserable than any peasant except a famine refugee, and that was very often the origin of the city 'coolie'.

It was possible, with luck or exceptional ability, to pass from one class to another, or with bad luck or folly, to sink to a lower level. The phenomenon in both directions was well known and accepted. A rich merchant could buy land, set up his family as landlords, educate his sons and get them, with luck and some ability, into the civil service and high up its ladder of promotion. There are many known examples of this ascent. A skilled artisan could save enough to set up his own business, a medium merchant could make big money, and even the poorest of the poor, by luck, or loot at a time of disorder or in the ranks of rebellion, could rise to the highest place. The founder of the Ming dynasty was a famine refugee before he became a monk, a bandit, a rebel and an emperor. This unregulated but real social mobility was a characteristic of Chinese society which sharply differentiates it from pre-modern Western society and from pre-revolutionary Russia.

There were also a large number of people, whole classes, which the old system did not include in its formal categories, probably because they had not formed in antiquity. These were miners (an hereditary occupation, as they often are elsewhere), charcoal burners, hunters, porters and boatmen, muleteers, itinerant Taoist priests who acted as fortune tellers, and a wide range of social flotsam, whom the Chinese called *po lo hu*, 'broken families'. This was a class which contributed manpower and devotion to many a rebellion, was truly subversive, having little to hope for in the existing system, and perhaps something to gain in times of disorder. They and their descendants to-day are not and never were peasants in any real sense; they did not own land, nor work it for others; they lived by a variety of occupations which were on the edge of the law and often beyond it.

All these varying elements have to be fitted into the new society, and must be re-educated to find their rightful place within it. They are not a new phenomenon, they have always been there, and they have characteristics which are not quickly effaced. It can be seen that in the first phase of the People's Republic there were tensions caused by this social transformation, and in certain cases the problems have not been easily solved. Since the end of the colonial empires, the overseas Chinese, coming from the two most southerly provinces of Kuangtung and Fukien, have often been exposed to persecution and discrimination in the newly independent countries. The People's Republic welcomed those who were driven out or deprived, or simply hoped for better times in the home country. But they have proved to be hard to assimilate; they had been raised and trained in a *bourgeois* society, came mainly from the small merchant class, and had remitted part of their savings to the family home in China. This custom was respected and encouraged by the Communist régime; it brought in foreign exchange, and the recipients were allowed to use the money. When migrants returned, they too expected to live in modest *bourgeois* comfort on the earnings they had sent home. This created a class of semi-privileged *petit bourgeois* who were a source of friction in the villages and small cities of the south.

Universal education, free, but with difficult hurdles to surmount, satisfied the aspirations of many and delighted the talented poor. But it also created a growing class of dissatisfied youth; those who were good, but not quite top-rate intellectual material, who could profit by secondary education with merit but were excluded from tertiary education, because there were not enough universities, nor staff to man them, in spite of massive expansion. Universal education produced too many young people who could profit by university education, but had to be shut out in favour of the small number of really first-class applicants. That many of the latter came from *bourgeois* origins or high Party membership (often one and the same thing) made the resentment of the excluded sharper. Moreover they did not find careers open to their range of ability; it requires only four or five years to raise up a vast number of clever school leavers, but in this time the factories and the industries which could employ them are still either in the blue-print stage or just under construction. Education outpaced the growth of the industrial economy which alone could produce the jobs for which the newly educated knew they had been trained, and to which increasingly they felt they had a right.

The Red Guards, the massive mobilisation of precisely this generation of dissatisfied youth, was the temporary, but rather hazardous solution provided by the Cultural Revolution, and used in that movement as a weapon to dislodge the opponents of Mao Tse-tung. Subsequently, when the Red Guards proved to be liable to break into quarrelling factions, the solution has been to attempt to obliterate the ancient distinction between town and country, literate and ignorant, by sending the young school leavers back to the country to become 'literate peasants' and raise the living standard of the communes, as also their economic activity, until the urban life holds no more attraction than life on the farm. The question which the future alone can answer is whether this extensive social engineering can overcome all the inherent differences in the constitution of the Chinese people, their traditional outlook, and their acquired social characteristics. A people who have admired and respected learning from time immemorial, and lived under the rule of the academically trained gentry, will readily take to education, achieve literacy and skills, but will certainly not be induced so easily to value these things less than their forefathers, who saw them as the only escape from the toil and stress of peasant life. Education was the mark of the higher class; now it is to be everyman's birthright. But what is it going to bring him in terms of a better life and wider opportunities? The risk is that it will be seen to qualify men for an urban job, and in China, as elsewhere, the draw of the great city is a real problem.

Unquestionably China is concerned with a great social transformation, the results of which are certain to be most significant and not only for China. Society in old China was not so rigid a structure as some propaganda might suggest, and social mobility has made revolution easier and less violent than in other, more class-bound societies. When Mao Tse-tung denounces privilege he finds a ready audience, because in China privilege without service or merit to justify it was regarded as transitory, undeserved, and amoral. The Cultural Revolution is also built upon some of the traditions of Chinese life while opposing others; above all it was a contest between differing views of what the Communist society should become, not whether there should be such a society at all.

'From the day Chiang Kai-shek started his counter-revolutionary war we said that we not only must defeat him but can defeat him.' (Mao Tse-tung)

The uneasy marriage of the CCP and the Nationalist Government barely survived the fight against their common enemy. Immediately the Japanese were defeated, it began to fall apart. Chiang Kai-shek ordered the Red Armies—the Eighth Route and the New Fourth— to remain where they were and await his instructions. Radio Yenan briskly responded: 'We consider you have given us a mistaken order. We are compelled to express ourselves to you that we firmly refute the order.'

The Red Army stormed and seized the capital of Manchuria and with it control of the railway north to the Russian border. Chiang started a terror campaign against all who dared criticise the government or the army and launched an offensive of about a million men against the Reds in the North China plain. For a time they were intoxicatingly successful, even capturing the stronghold of Yenan, a symbol, they felt, of final victory. But with the armies came the landlords and racketeers and the same old corruption, so they failed to win the hearts and minds of the common people. The harsh press-gang methods of recruitment were especially resented. Jack Belden travelled widely throughout China during this period, and one of his accounts says: 'Even more brutal than the KMT were the landlords. Very often they buried men alive who had engaged in the struggle for the reduction of rents. If they could not find these men they buried their families. According to the Anyang County Government, up to the time of my arrival four hundred men, women and children had been killed and buried alive in the 423 villages that had fallen into KMT hands.'

The Nationalists rejoiced too soon. A carefully planned counter sweep began in mid-1947; it found Chiang's forces over-extended and his base in Honan left denuded and vulnerable; the Red Armies moved in on it.

The final failure of the KMT was one of morale. Even with massive American military aid (equipment and ammunition) and advisers the soldiers remained ill-paid, ill-fed and ill-led; by 1947 they wanted only to give up the unequal struggle and regiments at a time went over or laid down their arms.

The final decisive battles were fought in 1948 and were nearly all won by the Reds. By early 1949 Peking and Tientsin had fallen; the Reds moved into Peking almost unopposed; American Derk Bodde watched them: 'Of chief interest was the Liberation Army itself. I counted over 250 heavy motor vehicles of all kinds—tanks, armoured cars, trucks mounted with machine guns . . . ambulances, jeeps and smaller vehicles. What made it specially memorable to Americans was the fact that it was primarily a display of American military equipment, virtually all of it captured or obtained by bribe from KMT forces. As the stream of trucks continued I heard several exclaim with wonder "Still more! Still more!"'[1]

Three months later, in April 1949, the Red Army made its vital crossing of the Yangtse River; 'to liberate all China', said the communiqué issued by Mao and Chu Teh. Nearly half a million KMT troops faced the Red Army with little to oppose their ships and planes. But the KMT had no heart to do anything to stop the Communists as they ferried themselves on wooden boats, junks and rafts. Nanking, Chiang's capital, fell. Southward they went, virtually unresisted, down almost to Hong Kong. The last vestige of his authority gone, Chiang crossed the Straits to Taiwan with the shattered remnants of his army, still regarding himself as the head of the Chinese Government, soon to return to the mainland. In 1972 he still so regards himself.

On 1 October Mao Tse-tung, standing where, for centuries, tradition decreed that emperors make their announcements, announced the founding of the People's Republic of China. 'We have united ourselves and defeated both foreign and domestic oppressors by the People's War of Liberation and we announce the founding of the People's Republic of China. Our nation will from now on enter the large family of peace-loving and freedom-loving nations of the world. . . . Our nation will never again be an insulted nation. We have stood up.'

The ghosts of opium clippers in Canton, of gunboats in the Yangtse, of Gordon, von Waldersee, Tojo and the war-lords were laid at last. China was her own man again. '*Fanshen*—We have turned over.'

onscripted soldiers for the KMT army. 'I often
w (as did many other foreigners) in the country-
le men yoked together like cattle with ropes
d round their necks being dragged along by
litary police.' (*The Other Side of the River* by
gar Snow)

ar scene late in 1948, the Huai-Hai campaign.

Mao Tse-tung proclaims the founding of the
People's Republic of China, 1 October 1949.

Notes and References

Chapter 2

1 Part of the text of the communiqué issued at the end of the
visit of President Richard Nixon of the United States of
America to China in February 1972:
'President Richard Nixon of the United States of America
visited the People's Republic of China at the invitation of
Premier Chou En-lai of the People's Republic of China from
February 21 to February 28, 1972 . . . The Leaders of the
People's Republic of China and the United States of America
found it beneficial to have this opportunity, after so many years
without contact, to present candidly to one another their
views on a variety of issues. They reviewed the international
situation in which important changes and great upheavals
are taking place and expounded their respective positions and
attitudes . . .
  The two sides reviewed the long-standing serious disputes
between China and the United States. The Chinese side re-
affirmed its position; the Taiwan question is the crucial question
obstructing the normalisation of relations between China and
the United States; the Government of the People's Republic
of China is the sole legal government of China; Taiwan is a
Province of China which has long been returned to the motherland; the liberation of Taiwan is China's internal affair in
which no other country has the right to interfere; and all US
forces and military installations must be withdrawn from
Taiwan. The Chinese Government firmly opposes any activities
which aim at the creation of "one China, one Taiwan", "one
China, two Goverments", "two Chinas", an "independent
Taiwan" or advocate that "the status of Taiwan remains to
be determined".'
  The US side declared: 'The United States acknowledges
that all Chinese on either side of the Taiwan Strait maintain
there is but one China and that Taiwan is a part of China.
The United States Government does not challenge that
position. It reaffirms its interest in a peaceful settlement of the
Taiwan question by the Chinese themselves. With this prospect
in mind, it affirms the ultimate objective of the withdrawal of
all US forces and military installations from Taiwan. In the
meantime, it will progressively reduce its forces and military
installations on Taiwan as the tension in the area diminishes . . .
They agree to facilitate the progressive development of trade
between their two countries. . . .
  'The two sides agreed that they will stay in contact through
various channels, including the sending of a senior US representative to Peking from time to time for concrete consultations
to further the normalisation of relations between the two
countries and continue to exchange views on issues of common
interest . . .
  'They believe that the normalisation of relations between the
two countries is not only in the interest of the Chinese and
American peoples but also contributes to the relaxation of
tension in Asia and the world.'

Chapter 5

1   *Life*, 30 April 1971.

Chapter 6

1   The Chinese comment on this, on 24 May 1969, is quietly disillusioned: 'Owing to historical conditions at the time no agreement was reached by the two sides on the boundary question, no redemarcation of the boundary between the two countries was made and no new equal treaty concluded . . . and this proletarian policy of Lenin failed to come true.'
  In 1954 Mao Tse-tung met Kruschev and Bulganin to discuss the status of Outer Mongolia but, as the Chairman said, 'the Russians refused to talk to us'

2   Writing in 1949, Dean Rusk, Truman's Secretary of State, confirmed that Stalin had assured the USA that he would continue recognition of the Nationalist Government.

3   George Moorad, *Lost Peace in China*, E. P. Dutton, 1949.

4   The four American diplomats who made the famous Mission to Yenan during the Anti-Japanese War made some illuminating comments on Sino–Soviet relations as they found them, revealing a Communist régime very far from Dean Rusk's Slavic Manchukuo. They discussed the too-powerful influence of American Ambassador Patrick Hurley and his misjudgment of the role of the Soviet Union in China.
  Emerson: 'Hurley was convinced the Chinese Communists would be told by Stalin to give in and to co-operate with the central government. But Mao was a Communist leader and prophet, and writer of doctrine in his own right . . . And therefore, even that early, they might have begun to develop, you see, in a separate way—not toward the Soviet Union—and the present split with the Soviet Union makes it quite obvious that their destiny did not lie irrevocably with the Soviet Union.'
  Davies: 'This was a very serious problem because we were committed then to Chiang in a situation which was highly fluid, which was disintegrating actually, and in which we were being committed to the losing side, and in which we were alienating the side that was going to win, and were forcing the side which was going to win into a relationship of alliance with the Soviet Union—which it may have been prepared to do anyway, but which in this case gave it no alternative but to go through with a tight tie-up with Russia. This was most unsound, and the repercussions from this have carried on for decades—up to today, of course.' (This and other quotations of these diplomats were taken from the television script of a documentary film made by Peter Davis in the USA, *Dixie Mission to Yenan*.)

Chapter 8

1   Robert Guillain, *Le Monde*, 25 March 1971.

Chapter 9

1   In his edition of *The Stilwell Papers*, Theodore White adds a footnote to this entry: 'For more about the relations between the Japanese and Chiang Kai-shek in the course of the war, see *Nazi–Soviet Relations 1939–1941* . . . published by the US

State Department. Matsuoka, Japan's Minister of Foreign Relations, told the Germans of his progress with Chiang Kai-shek in the spring of 1941.'

2 *Women of China*, Foreign Language Press, 1964.

Chapter 11

1 *Far Eastern Economic Review*, 18 March 1972.
2 Neil Taylor, *China Now*, February 1972.
3 *New China News*, March 1972.

Chapter 12

1 *Highlights of Chinese History*, Foreign Language Press, 1962.
2 *Short History of China 1840–1919*, Foreign Language Press, 1965.
3 W. H. Hall and W. S. Bernard, *The Nemesis in China*.
4 G. B. Smyth, 'The Crisis in China', *North American Review*.
5 W. Franke, *Hundred Years of Christian Revolution*, R. Oldenburg, 1958.
6 Agnes Smedly, *The Great Road*, Monthly Review Press, 1956.
7 *Highlights of Chinese History*, Foreign Language Press, 1962.
8 Mao Tse-tung, *Struggle in the Chingkang Mountains*, 1928.
9 *History of the Modern Chinese Revolution*, Foreign Language Press, 1959.
10 Jan Myrdal, *Report from a Chinese Village*, Pantheon, 1967.
11 Tibor Mende, *The Chinese Revolution*, Thames and Hudson, 1961.

Chapter 13

1 *China Reconstructs*, October 1971.

Chapter 15

1 It has been estimated that in 1950 there were about four million 'learned elements', of which only some 100 000 were highly qualified. In that year about 155 000 were attending higher education institutions: within a decade this number rose to 814 000. Existing research institutes of the foremost scientific body in China, the Academia Sinica, were steadily extended and new institutions founded. As early as 1963 there were about 700 institutes attached to the Academia Sinica and the Academies of Agriculture and Medicine. Today, there are more, and the number of university research departments has greatly increased.
2 *China in Transition*, Foreign Language Press, 1955.
3 W. G. Sewell, *I Stayed in China*, Allen & Unwin, 1966.
4 Editorial, *Red Flag*, 1967.
5 *China Now*, May 1971.
6 R. L. Whitehead, *Eastern Horizon*, June 1971.

Chapter 16

1 A student paper stated in 1919: 'Throughout the world like the voice of a prophet had gone the word of Woodrow Wilson, strengthening the weak and encouraging the strong. And the Chinese have listened and they, too, have heard . . . When the news of the peace conference finally reached us we were greatly shocked. We awoke at once to the fact that foreign nations were still selfish and militaristic and were all great liars.
2 Stuart Gelder, *The Chinese Communists*, Gollancz, 1946.
3 J. Bertram, *The North China Front*, 1939.
4 M. Endicott, *Five Stars Over China*, 1953.
5 W. Hinton, *China's Continuing Revolution*, China Policy Study Groups, 1969.
6 W. G. Sewell, *I Stayed in China*, Allen & Unwin, 1966.

Chapter 18

1 D. Bodde, *Peking Diary: 1948–1949, A Year of Revolution*, Henry Schurman, 1950.

Bibliography

A General History of Nineteenth and Twentieth Century China

Clubb, O. E., *Twentieth Century China*, Columbia University Press, 1964.

Fitzgerald, C. P., *Birth of Communist China*, Penguin, 1964.

McAleavy, Henry, *A Modern History of China*, Weidenfeld & Nicholson, 1967.

Pelissier, R., *The Awakening of China, 1793–1949*, Secker & Warburg, 1967.

Roper, Myra, *China in Revolution, 1911–1949*, Edward Arnold, 1971.

Schurmann, F. and Schell, O., (eds.), *China Readings: Imperial China, Republican China, Communist China*, Penguin, 1969.

Foreign Language Press Publications, Peking

A Concise History of China, 1964.

From Emperor to Citizen (an autobiography of the last Emperor of China), 1965.

History of the Modern Chinese Revolution, 1959.

The Revolution of 1911, 1962.

A Short History of China, 1840–1919, 1965.

Soong Ching-ling, *The Struggle for the New China*, 1953.

Thirty Years of the Communist Party of China, 1959.

B China and the West

Chang Hsin-hai, *China and America*, Simon & Schuster, 1965.

Fairbank, J. R., and Teng, S. Y., *China's Response to the West*, Oxford University Press, 1954.

Tang Tsou, *America's Failure in China*, Chicago University Press, 1963.

US State Department, *US Relations with China*, Far Eastern Series, 1949.

Waley, A., *The Opium War Through Chinese Eyes*, Allen & Unwin, 1958.

White, T., (ed.), *The Stilwell Papers*, MacDonald, 1948.

C China and Russia

Brandt, C., *Stalin's Failure in China*, Cambridge, Massachusetts, 1958.

Clark, G., *In Fear of China*, Lansdowne Press, 1967.

Mehrnert, K., *Peking and Moscow*, Mentor Books, 1963.

Wei, H., *China and Soviet Russia*, Princeton University Press, 1956.

D China and Japan

Butow, R. J., *Japan's Decision to Surrender*, Stanford University Press, 1967.

Chian, Hsiao, *China But Not Cathay*, Pilot Press, 1942.

Crow, C., *Japan's Dream of World Empire*, Harper Bros, 1942.

Timperley, H. J., *What War Means*, Gollancz, 1938.

E Peasant Rebellions and Peasant Life

Crook, I. and D., *First Years of the Yangyi Commune*, Routledge Kegan Paul, 1966.

Harrison, J., *The Communists and Chinese Peasant Rebellions*, Gollancz, 1970.

Hinton, W., *Fanshen*, Monthly Review Press, 1966.
Johnson, Chalmers, *Peasant Nationalism and Communist Power: The Emergence of Revolutionary China, 1937–45*, Stanford University Press, 1963.
Meadows, T. T., *The Chinese and Their Rebellions*, Stanford University Academic Reprint, 1954, first published 1856.
Michael, F., *The Taiping Rebellion*, University of Washington Press, 1966.
Myrdal, J., *Report from a Chinese Village*, Penguin, 1967.
Purcell, V., *Boxer Uprising*, Cambridge University Press, 1963.

F   Mao Tse-Tung and the Rise of the Communist Party
Belden, J., *China Shakes the World*, Harper Bros., 1949.
Devillers, P., *What They Really Said—Mao*, MacDonald, 1967.
Gelder, S., *The Chinese Communists*, Gollancz, 1946.
Lewis, J. W., *Major Doctrines of Communist China*, W. Norton, 1964.
Poems of Mao Tse-tung, and *More Poems of Mao Tse-tung*, Eastern Horizon, H.K.
North, R. C., *Chinese Communism*, World University Library, 1966.
Schram, S., *The Political Thought of Mao Tse-tung*, Penguin, 1966.
Snow, Edgar, *Red Star Over China*, Gollancz, 1963.

Foreign Language Press Publications, Peking
Five Articles by Chairman Mao Tse-tung, 1968.
On the Long March with Chairman Mao, 1970.
Selected Readings from the Works of Mao, 1967.
Selected Works of Mao Tse-tung, 1961.

G   The Intellectuals
Chow, T. T., *The May 4 Movement*, Harvard University Press, 1960.
Flesch P., *The Great Cultural Revolution in China*, Asian Research Centre, Melbourne, 1970.
MacFarquhar, R., *The Hundred Flowers*, Stevens, Paris, 1960.
Robinson, Joan, *The Cultural Revolution*, Penguin, 1969.
Wright, Mary, *The Last Stand of Chinese Conservatism, 1862–74*, Stanford University Press, 1957.
Yang, Y. C., *The Chinese Intellectuals and the West*, University of North Carolina Press.

H   Living in China: Books of General Interest
Cusack, Dymphna, *Chinese Women Speak*, Angus & Robertson, 1958.
Greene, F., *The Wall Has Two Sides*, Jonathan Cape, 1966.
Mackerras, C., and Hunter, N., *China Observed*, Thomas Nelson Australia, 1967.
Roper, Myra, *China, The Surprising Country*, Heinemann, 1966.
Sewell, W. G., *I Stayed in China*, Allen & Unwin, 1966.
Snow, Edgar, *The Other Side of the River*, Gollancz, 1963.
Suyin, Han, *The Crippled Tree; Birdless Summer; A Mortal Flower*, (trilogy), Jonathan Cape, 1965–8.
Terrill, R., *800 000 000 The Real China*, Heinemann, 1972.

Additional Books on China and Japan

MacNair, H. F., and Lach, D., *Modern Far Eastern International Relations*, van Nostrand, 1955.

Masamichi Royama, *The Foreign Policy of Japan*, Japanese Institute of Foreign Relations, 1941.

Tatsuji Takeuchi, *War and Diplomacy in the Japanese Empire, 1869–1934*, Doubleday, 1935.

Chinese Periodicals in English

China Pictorial (monthly)

China Reconstructs (monthly)

Peking Review (weekly)

English Periodicals

China Quarterly, London.

Eastern Horizon, Hong Kong.

Far Eastern Economic Review, Hong Kong.

INDEX

Kailan Mining, 42, 55
Kaiping Mines, 42
Kang Yu-wei, 41, 201
Karakhan Declaration and Manifesto, 73
Kashgar, 73
Kissinger, H., 29, 67
Kobodo, 72
Ko Lao Hui Secret Society, 141
Korea, 25, 27, 33, 72, 84, 85, 88, 90, 93, 94, 101
Kosygin, 63, 72
Kruschev, 16, 59, 60, 64, 65, 69, 72, 75, 232
Kuang Hsu, 201
KMT, *see* Kuomintang
Kuomintang, 219, 221; and the CCP, 98, 158, 177, 180–1, 204, 227–8; and Japan, 181; and the May Fourth Movement, 202; and the peasants, 206, 223; and the Soviet Union, 74, 80; and Sun Yat-sen, 23, 178; and the United States, 25, 27, 34, 58; *see also* Chiang Kai-shek
Kuo Mo-jo, 32

Landlords, 152, 155
Land Reform, 118, 120–1, 157, 142, 206, 221; *see* Agriculture
Language, Japanese influence on, 85
Lao Pai Hsing, 114
Latin America, 15, 67
Lattimore, Professor Owen, 66
League of Nations, 43
Lenin, *see* Marxism-Leninism
Liang Chi-chao, 201
Liang Hsiu-ying, 190
Liaotung Peninsula, 94
Liberation War, 222, 228
Li Hung-chang, 41, 49, 72, 93, 101
Li Li-san, 203, 204
Lin Piao, 75, 120–1, 162, 187, 189, 199, 204
Lin Tse-hsu, Commissioner, 40, 46
Li Ta-chao, 201, 202
Literature, 172, 186
Liu Jen-ching, 202
Liu Kwei-wu, 139
Liu Shao-chi, 188, 189, 190, 198, 204, 206
Long March, The, 145–6, 158–62, 203, 232
Lu Chih, 138, 152
Ludden, Ray, 43
Lu Hsun, 201
Lüshan, *see* Port Arthur
Lu Ting-yi, 184

MacArthur, General D., 27
Manchu dynasty, 24, 177

Manchuria, 72; and the CCP, 227; and Japan, 43, 84–5, 94, 95, 102; and the Soviet Union, 60, 72–3, 75, 80
Manual labour, 185–6, 189–90, 195, 196
Mao Tse-tung, Chapter 16 and throughout the text
Marco Polo Bridge Incident, 102
Marshall, General, 44, 181
Marxism-Leninism, 232; and Japan 87; and Mao Tse-tung, 23, 67, 123–4, 185, 201–3; and the peasants, 140–1; and revisionism, 188; and Yen Fu, 22; attitude to China, 73; China's attitude to, 74, 82, 176, 178–9, 181
Matsuoka, 233
May Fourth Movement, 95, 201–2, 209
May Thirtieth Incident, 203
Medicine, 39, 123, 133; *see* Acupuncture, Barefoot doctors
Mehrhert, Klaus, 63, 64
Mencius, 115, 118, 138, 147
Mende, Tibor, 145
Militarism, 227–8
Military science, 22, 49, 50
Mill, John Stuart, 22
Ming period, 84
Missionaries, 21, 24, 25, 53
Mission to Yenan, 28
Mongolia, 72, 80, 84, 85, 95, 232
Montesquieu, 22
Moorad, George, 75
Moulton, Rev. Dr, 47
Movements, self-strengthening, 41
Mukden, 75
Music, 164, 173; *see* Opera
Mutual Alliance Assistance, 63
Myrdal, Jan, 121, 144

Nanking Treaty, 21, 40
Napoleon, 15
'National capitalists', 221, 222
Nationalism, and Sun Yat-sen, 23; and the revolutionaries, 177; and the people, 179–80; *see* Kuomintang
Nationalist Party, *see* Kuomintang
Needham, Professor Joseph, 122
Nixon, Richard, and Japan, 89; and the Soviet Union, 67; visit of to China, 15, 28–30, 37, 44, 165, 231
Nuclear weapons, 37
Nung, 120, 146

Okinawa, 87, 90
Okinawa Reversion Agreement, 90
On the Chinese Revolution and the CCP, 204
On Contradiction, 204
On the Correct Handling of Contradictions Among the People, 182, 185, 186